How to Start a Fire Under the Sea:

Volume III of The Travels of Senator & Wendy V

- © 2009 by Wendy V. All rights reserved. No part of this publication may be reproduced or transmitted in any form or by any means, electronic or mechanical, including photocopy, recording, or any information storage and retrieval system, without the prior written consent of the author and/or publisher.

- cover photography © 2009 by Wendy V.

ISBN: 978-0-99150-932-4

for Senator—

...What are we listening to tonight?...

"Like all great travelers, I have seen more than I remember, and remember more than I have seen."

~Benjamin Disraeli

Table of Contents

Introduction	i
Missouri Loves Company	1
(But It's a Dry Heat)	17
Death's Door, and Other Fun Portals	59
Welcome Back	77
Song of the South	97
Afterword	133

Author's Note

See Author's Note, *How to Read a Compass in the Dark.*

Introduction

I am not sure why the burning urge to travel embeds itself in some of us. You could blame it on escapism, except for the fact that I love my home, and can easily be accused of hermitude at regular intervals. Perhaps, then, it is simple curiosity-- that unquenchable thirst to know, to see, to experience, to evaluate, and ultimately, to recall fondly. Maybe the journey teaches us things about other people; it certainly teaches us things about ourselves. I sometimes get the sense that traveling grows me, not just in the hips and thighs, but as a human being, simultaneously an inferior speck and a divinely-inspired creative force. Then again, maybe I just like a good vacation like everyone else.

These are the chronicles of the third two-year cycle of our travels. At the beginning of this period, I took on a new job, which redefined the vacation parameters a bit, but it generally worked out. We also knocked out another chunk of states on the good old U.S. of A. map. (Remind me to get out the colored pencils and update that.) So grab a tent peg and your flea market cash, and come along for the ride.

~Wendy V
May 2008

Chapter 1
Missouri Loves Company:
Early October 2007

The timing of events in my life never ceases to amaze me, and the summer of 2007 was no exception. Senator and I entered our fifth year together, and made plans for a road trip to his beloved Southwest. Anyone who knows me knows that my heart is in the exact opposite end of the country, (which could explain our Midwest address,) but I was anxious to visit the mountains, deserts, and canyons that I had not seen since I was a teenager. Of course, by now I would probably follow that boy to the moon. Hhmmm.. *I wonder what their visitor center looks like...*

In classic Wendy V style, I suggested an itinerary and mapped out a route. In classic Senator style, he smiled, nodded, and then demanded to know when I planned to shop for a decent pair of hiking boots. Apparently my $4.00 Target specials were not going to cut it. All right, all right. I would find suitable shoes. After all, I needed a preliminary line of defense against all of the rattlesnakes and scorpions that I was sure would attack at the first opportunity.*

The agreed upon dates for the road trip fell in October, a wonderful month in which to travel. The late fall keeps the kids in school and the wimpy campers at home, or at least safely tucked in their 7-mile-per-gallon RVs, complete with satellite reception. With months to go before we had to think about packing, we spent a fairly calm summer at home. We even managed to landscape more of the yard and remodel the bathroom. The fact that I was only working a part-time nanny gig helped , but in August I would continue my part-time high school security job.

Sooner than expected, August 1st rolled around. I went back to school and met with the other security team members to plan out the year. At some point I was pulled away by an administrator. When I went to see him, to my complete shock, he offered me a full time teaching position. *What?! As in a 'big girl job'?* Essentially, the job I had beat my brains out chasing for years just fell into my lap. My head spinning, I accepted.

There are two ways one can get hired for a teaching position. The first way is the method that happens to normal people, where a formal application is followed by a series of interviews and a leisurely three months of preparing lesson plans and one's classroom arrangement, while gently phasing out a previous job. The second way is the way that could only happen to me.

---

*My mother tells a story about traveling in the South and stopping at a rest area with a giant billboard warning about rattlesnakes. In her legendary wisdom, she reasoned that, if the sign was that big, the snakes probably were too. She decided to hold it. Smart gal. There are many places to *not* get bitten by a snake, but *there* would surely be the worst!

On a Thursday, I returned to school as security personnel, and twenty-four hours later I was a teacher. I also still had nanny obligations. How was I going to tell the family I worked for that I was quitting? Then there was the fact that the class I would be teaching was changing rooms over the summer.

It looked something like this: after the interview, I was basically given a key and a hearty "good luck". When I unlocked the 100ºF room, there was a sour smell, accompanied by a literal pile of furniture and mismatched boxes in the middle of the floor. I could not locate a pen, let alone a discernible curriculum. As the sweat poured down my face and salted my lips, I had just two thoughts-- hello students in just ten days, and goodbye October vacation.

Still, I was ecstatic as I rushed home to tell Senator that, for once, our vacation was getting messed up for a good reason. He too was thrilled, and then changed expressions as he asked me if I got the message from the man I worked for as a nanny. "No," I cut in, "but I need to talk to them anyway, because I have to quit them this Monday already..."

"Well," he paused, "You better just listen to it for yourself..."

Allow me here, Reader, to paraphrase the message that awaited me. "Hey, Wendy. Um, this is Ray[*]. Listen, Carla[†] freaked out and tried to say I hit her, and now I'm in jail for the weekend. Can you stay with the kids until this is straightened out?"

What?! You have got to be kidding me! Before I could even think, I was grabbing my toothbrush and pillow and heading out the door, kissing Senator goodbye between worrying about the kids and swearing at the stupidity of the parents. I passed a few days of barely-controlled chaos with three little children as they

---

[*]Names have been changed to protect the innocent.
[†]Names have been changed to protect the idiotic.

tried to understand their ridiculous predicament. Sunday night I returned home, exhausted, and completely unaware that I was a teacher until Senator reminded me. *Oh, right. That.* Thus, my week leading up to the first day of school went something like this:

> **7:30am-12:00pm:** fulfill previous security commitments, since they did not expect this either
>
> **12:00pm-2:00pm:** dive into the pile of crap in my classroom and try desperately to arrange/decipher it, between guzzling gallons of water in an attempt to stay hydrated, lest maintenance workers follow the stench to find my lifeless body four days later
>
> **2:00pm-8:30pm:** try to restore some semblance of order to the resulting mess of the family for which I nannied/interview new potential nanny/remind myself that I shouldn't feel guilty about the timing of my new job
>
> **8:30pm-11:00pm:** develop/fake a semester outline and the first few lesson plans
>
> **11:00pm-11:05pm:** "me time" (because I'm told this is important)
>
> **11:05pm-12:00am:** remember that I have the greatest guy in the world, and thank him for that fact

And so it was, that the Southwest would have to wait until the following June. Stupid dream job.

As the whirlwind semester got underway, I began to plot ways to sneak in a quick trip somewhere... anywhere. Scanning the calendar, I saw that we had a three-day weekend approaching in October for Columbus's birthday. Those close to me (as well as every student for the rest of my career) know that I abhor Christophoro Columbo. Why we honor a pirate who used religion as an excuse to invade the native population is beyond me. In fact, my favorite Columbus reference is on a shirt that depicts Native North Americans above the line "Homeland Security-- Fighting Terrorism Since 1492". Enough said.

Nevertheless, three days off would be enough time to run down to Missourah for a quick visit with my sister. I have to be honest. My sister's decision to remain in the Show-Me State after her graduation concerns me on some level. Don't get me wrong. That she has friends, contacts, and a job that she loves pleases me greatly, but what are the *long-term* effects of being a transplanted Yankee?[*]

Though she is reluctant to admit it, Heidi's speech is tinged with Missourian. Words like 'counselor' have adopted the superfluous t to become 'count-selor'. Syllables, though not fully drawled, hang on a littler longer than we are comfortable with in Chicagoland. I'm concerned is all I'm saying. What if she starts cookin' sweet potato pie? And grits? Worse, she might trade in organic herbal teas for sweet tea, or even begin pricing a rebel flag to hang in her living room window. Yes, it was good that we were going down to check on Little Sis.

We made our plans with a very enthusiastic Heidi, who volunteered to guide us through the local woods. It sounded like a perfect autumn retreat. I envisioned the hills in the morning mist, the sunlight highlighting the transforming reds, oranges, and golds. Cozy sweatshirts. Hot coffee. Crisp, clean air perfumed with cool forest.

Or not. How were we supposed to predict that our fall weekend would see temperatures in the upper 80s?[†] Nevertheless, we were excited to see Heidi and her new

---

[*]Incidentally, for those of you who are quick to point out that *technically* Missouri is a 'border state' and not actually part of the South, I give you the Ozarks and Branson.

[†]We later learned that we were not the only ones disappointed by the blazing October heat. Runners in the Chicago Marathon dropped out or passed out until officials finally told them to go home. The lesson here is that it is always best to play it safe-- never go running. Ever.

apartment. We only had two and a half days, so we had to make the most of it. At an ambitious and starry 5:00am, we left for Missouri.

The trip through Illinois was reasonably pleasant, dotted with the construction-orange that has become our unofficial state color. After a lifetime on Illinois interstate highways, the barricades, signs, and flashing lights are notable symbols of warm weather, like fresh-cut grass and fluttering robins. After a few hours the St. Louis Arch was in view, and we crossed the mighty Mississippi into Heidi territory. Now it was time to buckle down and get serious.

My sister had warned us about Missouri drivers, and it is no exaggeration to say that they rival those of Boston for some of the worst I have encountered. A primer is here provided, should you ever find yourself cruising merrily along I-44:

> **Rule #1:** Posted speed limits are just that-- limits. They should be met only in dire emergencies. All other highway travel should take place at a maximum 55mph pace.
> **Rule #2:** Cell phone conversations-- mandatory. Unsuccessful multitasking attempts while driving and phoning-- even better.
> **Rule #3:** Never use a turn signal. This especially applies when it becomes necessary to change lanes at the last moment. An exception to this rule, however, is permitted when one is in the right lane, with the right blinker on, and no turn-off is in sight. In such cases, the signal must be left on for a minimum of ten miles.
> **Rule #4:** Though no stop sign is present, one must stop on an entrance ramp prior to merging onto the interstate. (This also provides an appropriate time to take in the delightful scenery.)

Rule #5: When on the interstate, and vehicles are attempting to merge into your lane, under no circumstances should you move over to the left lane. (This also encourages those speed-demon foreigners from Illinois to follow Rule #4.)

In the early afternoon, we arrived at Heidi's apartment. I was glad to see that it reflected her personality. Vibrant red accents were set against classic black, white, and silver tones. I thought for a moment, with a slight pang of regret, of the Chinese fan that I had wanted to buy her when Senator and I were in New York. *If only I had listened to the angry shopkeeper. Perhaps she was right. Perhaps I really only needed to open one...* Alas, there would be no fan.

We settled in to relax and cool off. The mercury soared and the afternoon humidity increased. We still wanted to take a short hike, but it was a relief when Heidi mentioned that she had a few air conditioned stops to make first. First on the agenda-- Walmart.

Oh, come on. How can you go to the same region of our great land that gave birth to Sam Walton's dream without visiting one of the spawns of the beast? Actually, the reason I mention it is due to the irony of the matter. The Springfield, Missouri, Walmart was even cheaper than its Illinois counterparts, but had an unbelievable selection of gourmet and health foods. Cheeses I had not seen since Greenwich Village, and four different brands of soy milk lined the shelves. Wow-- talk about the best of both worlds! I guess it pays (literally) to live in a college town.

When the wonder of Walmart had subsided, we psyched ourselves up for a walk through the local nature center. Two minutes along the path I was soaked in the pits. We were also not used to breathing water, that is, Missouri air. Senator and I both loathe Illinois humidity, but this was even more intense, compounded by the fact that our lungs were already accustomed to a drier autumn. I soldiered on like a two-pack-per-day smoker. Heidi, on the other hand, lilted ahead, apparently unaffected. *So she is turning southern, after all!*

When we came to a small stream, all three of us froze. There, drinking calmly from the brook, was a doe and one of her fawns. Though we see deer year-round at home, they usually sprint away at the first sight of a human. These creatures, however, went about their business within twenty feet of us, unfazed. I hoped that they were not so tame as to endanger themselves.

We looked to the other side of the stream and a second fawn was cautiously making his way down to the water's edge. He showed a little more concern than the others, alternating glances between us and his mother. After each look toward her, he took a step or two toward his drink, reassured. Eventually he joined them. Yet again, I was amazed at the subtle complexity of the animal kingdom.

My introspective moment was disrupted when Heidi told us about some idiots who were recently in trouble for deer hunting in the nature center. That figures. I could just picture that hillbilly conversation. "Hey, Jeb, wanna' go huntin' tomorra'?"

"Sure, Cletus. What fer?"

"Oh, I was sposin' we could find us some deers."

"Yeah? Great! I know jus' the spot if ya'll don't wanna' work too hard. You won't even need yer camo!" I sighed. I was just starting to think that maybe I had misjudged Missouri. No worry there.

We concluded our walk and piled into the air-conditioning of the car. It had already been a long day, and we were hungry. Somewhat surprisingly, near Heidi's home was an Indian restaurant. She had yet to experience Indian cuisine, so we decided it was high time we introduce her. The food at Gem of India was excellently seasoned and consistent with what we loved about New York and Chicago Indian dishes. I have no idea what attracts people from the other side of the world to the American Bible Belt, but I am glad they bring their traditional flavors with them.

After dinner we took a short drive around town before heading back to Heidi's apartment. You would think we would have had one of those all-night fun fests that sisters sometimes share when they have not seen each other in a long time, but the night turned out somewhat differently. After visiting and looking at Heidi's latest photography portfolio, I suggested we honor that age-old October tradition of watching *It's the Great Pumpkin, Charlie Brown*. As long as we were still pretending it felt like fall, I popped in the other classic, *The Legend of Sleepy Hollow*. Ten minutes into it, I had the 'sleepy' part down pat. I guess you can only party so long on five hours' sleep and a 5:00am departure time. Oh, rats!

Sunday morning started out with little more ambition than the night before. We all chatted casually while Heidi got ready for church. I promised her a delicious brunch when she got back, but in the meantime, I opted for some hardcore vacation laziness. Deciding that I was at least capable of reading a chapter, I checked back in with the weighty Einstein biography I had started dragging around the week before. For the record, 500+ page tales of eccentric physicists are not my general weekend excursion reading choice, but I was on a roll. In short, the man was brilliant, socially conscious, driven, passionate, humorous, and a real jerk if you had the misfortune to become one of his wives. Still, his is a fascinating story, if for no other reason than his astounding thoroughness in keeping a secret. I will let you discover it for yourself.

Einstein finished another affair, and I finished reading. The time had come to prepare my decadent good-for-the-soul stuffed French toast. I rattled around the apartment-sized kitchen searching for pans, selecting knives, and making a generally satisfying mess. Senator offered to help a few times, but I was in too deep. *No Baby, it might be too dangerous. You stay in the living room, and come rescue me if I'm not out in twenty minutes.* For whatever reason, the smaller the kitchen I work in, the greater the mess I make. *There's an equation for you to figure out, Einstein.*

When my furious tornado ceased, I plated fresh fruit with cinnamon, a variety of hard and soft cheeses, and scrumptious, messy stuffed French toast. Heidi arrived home just in time. I lit the candles, always essential to enhancing taste. I could feel the sweaty blast of heat when she opened the front door. Nothin' like a good, hot brunch on a steamy, blistering day! We raised our glasses in a juice toast: "Next year somewhere cool!"

The afternoon entertainment now loomed. Senator, always cognizant of his history-geek girlfriend, had read about a local settlement containing the "oldest house in Springfield". It sounded like a Simpsons gag, but we were game, so our threesome set off. We drove a few miles and found an obscure entrance, with a confusingly marked parking lot. We parked and began walking down a paved road toward what looked like a farm.

As we approached, we realized that it was not our farm. We still had farther to go. By now it seemed that every drink of water we took spilled right out of our pores. I was reminded of the cartoons where someone is shot, and then drinks a glass of water, only to watch it run onto the ground. I could only hope I was burning some of the French toast off my thighs.

Finally, we reached our destination. Several log buildings were scattered between old, sprawling trees. It looked like a perfect spot for a picnic. What it did not look like was a home that was open for tours, as the listed information had promised. The only part that was open was an adjacent garden, hedged in by dense evergreens. For an exorbitant price, you could go poke around there. No, thank you. We'll be content to just peek in the windows of the locked buildings. Of course, I also tried to jiggle every door latch, just in case.*

No doors budged, and our water supply was dwindling. Senator, Heidi, and I glanced at one another with a unanimous, "Let's blow this joint." We started back, noting gingerly that we could have saved distance if a certain field was not locked off. Except for the exercise, the journey to the oldest house in Springfield was a bust. The afternoon was not a loss, however, as we were now headed to 'the trashiest thrift store in Springfield'.

One thing that surprises visitors to Springfield is the complete diversity within the city. Old established families, college kids, and immigrants from around the globe all make up significant percentages of the population. This, in turn, leads to a highly varied cityscape. While most towns have some neighborhoods which are better than others, Springfield's economic disparity is especially apparent. Large, lovely homes in meticulous shape on one end of town are contrasted sharply with almost shack-like dwellings on the other side. Everything in between is, well, everything in between.

So, with our perky blond tour guide at the wheel, we explored the many regions of Springfield. When we stopped at a red light and noticed the handsome sign on the crummy building nearby, we had to stop. "Flea market-- everything half off". Heidi maneuvered her compact car into an even more compact lot, careful not to plunge into one of the many pot holes. We climbed out of the car and approached the door. Coming in after us was a man the size of all three of us. Disturbingly, he was

---

*This actually worked once when I was stalking a deserted Victorian mansion in Joliet. I had one foot in the door when some well-meaning 'friends' barred me from going any further. I reasoned that it's hardly breaking-and-entering if you are researching, but alas, they outnumbered me.

wearing a tank top made for a man of normal stature. Billowing mounds of flesh poured out of every available exit in the shirt.

Once inside, everything was, indeed, priced to sell, as the cigarette chomping, fried-haired darlin' at the register reminded us merrily. I hated to think it, but she bore an uncanny resemblance to the 'before' girl on a say-no-to-meth poster that we had at my high school. Nevertheless, we had dollars in our pockets, and many wood-frame shelves of junk to explore. We picked our way through ugly knick-knacks, forsaken collectibles, dirty pillows and linens, and all other manner of flea market fare. When we heard children whining, or spotted a fine patron blowing smoke rings while shopping, we would abruptly switch directions, mid-aisle. It was like a game.

Believe it or not, the venture yielded two distinct treasures. First, I stumbled across odd plates and bowls that matched the pattern of our kitchen dishes. What would you pay for these lovely and hard-to-find pieces? Don't answer yet. My second prize was an assortment of various editions of the children's book *Heidi*. What better housewarming gift for my sister? *Now* what would you pay? Ten dollars? Fifteen dollars? Try $5.50, and we'll throw in a lesson in Springfield subculture for free.

We made our way through the Missourians and to the car with our acquisitions. Negotiating our way out of the lot, we continued on our extended driving tour of the city. It seemed every other block held a college or church. From megachurches to minichurches, Christianity comes in every possible flavor here: Methodist, Episcopalian, Lutheran, Pentecostal, Evangelical, T.V. Evangelical, Baptist, Southern Baptist, Baptist Who Cannot Get Along With Those of the Regular or Southern Variety, etc. As Heidi so eloquently puts it, "If this is the Bible Belt, Springfield is the buckle." Amen, Sister.

In keeping with our when-in-Rome agenda, it was now time to indulge in the feeding frenzy that is dinner at Lambert's.

Rather, it was time to put our name on the wait list to get a table at Lambert's. Lambert's is one of those signature restaurants that earns its reputation for quirkiness. Their slogan, "Home of the Throwed Roll" refers to their tradition of whipping hot, homemade rolls to the table of anyone who signals the Thrower.

The customer's receiving skills are then put to the test. While most buns find their way into grateful hands, it is not unusual for the errant bread to go sailing into a light fixture, onto the floor, or atop the beehive of the lady in the booth behind you. Lambert's other claim to fame is their select, standard family style refillables. Servers wander the aisles with trucker-sized bowls of macaroni, fried potatoes, and fried okra, ready to dish a dollop out to your table.

The décor is retro-kitschy and fun, and everyone genuinely seems to have a good time there, including the staff. Hot melt-in-your-mouth rolls and vegetables fried until they cross the line into junk food-- now that's southern hospitality. So, Reader, if you ever make it to Springfield, get your buns to the Home of the Throwed Rolls. Tell 'em Wendy V sent you. It won't get you a table any sooner, but it will make me feel good.

With our sides sore from laughing, and our arteries thoroughly clogged, we returned to the apartment. The next day Heidi would have to get up for work, and we would be on our way. I knew the time would go far too fast; it always does. We passed a couple of hours talking about our plans for the rest of the year, and when we would see each other again. Ironically, driving to see my sister had suddenly made her seem farther away. I guess I had been pretending she was only an hour away whenever I spoke with her on the phone. Now, after the realization of the road trip and seeing firsthand the vastly changed landscape, it hit me that she had actually moved away. Hhmmm. I would have to ponder this one another time. I nestled down in our air mattress bunk, wishing the night could last longer.

Monday, our final morning, we attempted to visit with Heidi as she bustled around getting ready for work. The entire weekend had been a blur. In that same spirit, out she darted, and an hour later we were on our own way. Before going home, however, Senator allowed me to drag him to the local Civil War site.

Wilson's Creek Battlefield is the out-of-the-way and poorly marked historical site that commemorates the first Civil War battle fought west of the Mississippi River. In 1861, Missouri held the strange border state position of technically remaining loyal to the Union while having very strong Confederate sympathies, bringing about regular clashes with Lincoln's boys. At Wilson's Creek, both sides suffered considerable casualties, as reflected in the name of Bloody Hill. In the end, it was a Southern victory.

Using three different maps, we eventually deciphered the route, interweaving between various construction zones. We parked the car and walked up to the front door. A kind lady greeted us, and then explained that we were in the wrong location. Though somehow related to Wilson's Creek Battlefield, this structure was not part of the grounds. In fact, it was on private property. *How did the two armies even find this place?*

A mile or so down the road was the true battlefield. It was starting to sprinkle as we walked into the visitor center. Modest admission prices were listed on the board behind the park ranger. As I dug through my purse for two adults' worth of entrance fees, the ranger spoke. "One adult and... how old are *you*?" He aimed a strong index finger directly at me, but that did not stop me from looking behind myself. Nope, no one there.

"Who? Me?" I laughed. "Oh, I'm definitely an adult." I forked over the cash as my inner voice accused me of telling a half-truth. *At least, I am on some days...*

Senator offered his point of support. "Yeah, she's a history teacher!" This is why I love looking younger than my

14

true age. 1.) It gives me hope that I have inherited my grandma's genes and I will age well. 2.) I get to watch people squirm when they realize how far off they were. I then get to decide how long to let them squirm before absolving them with some politely excusing comment. 3.) If I really get a live one, who thinks that I am a minor, I can hang all over my older boyfriend and enjoy the uncomfortable and disapproving looks. As I always tell my students when they ask my age, "I'm old enough to not have to answer that question."

We did the short version of the visitor center and returned to the car. It was raining harder now, and we were somewhat pressed for time, so we opted for the driving tour. Even at a cool 20 mph, it feels strange to breeze by the points that once required hours of tiresome marching to reach. Let it be said that this is not the preferred method of experiencing history, but I take what I can get.

We continued along the loop through the park, careful not to squish the dopey turtles that occasionally crossed the road, or the dopey joggers that more than occasionally got on my nerves. Seriously-- who wakes up in the morning and says to herself, "Wow. What a lovely overcast morn. Sure looks like rain. I must take advantage of said approaching squall and go for a run. I think today I'll drive out to an obscure historical site so I can race the cars on the park road while learning about Nineteenth Century military strategy. Okay, now where did I put my earth-tone spandex and camouflage sweatbands?"

I'll just come clean and say it. If you are a jogger who acts like 90% of the joggers I encounter (especially near the suburbs,) I do not like you. Sorry, but it's true. This does not mean that I will try to run you off the road, but it also does not mean that I will try *not* to. Please find a nice sidewalk and some brightly colored clothing, and lose the ridiculously intense stare, and perhaps then we can begin to peacefully coexist. Maybe.

We completed our tour of Wilson's Creek and found our way back to the interstate and the Missouri-trained drivers. The drive home was pleasant, if relatively boring. For example, we had agreed to stop for dinner on the road once we noticed something interesting. Just two hours from home, still nothing had materialized, prompting a big bag of gas station potato chips to become dinner. We alternated greasy and clean hands to corral awol crumbs and sip from the family water bottle. *Oh yeah. This is living, Baby.*

Before too long, we were back at our humble abode. I was satisfied to have seen my sister and her new surroundings. I was also okay with the fact that it would be another eight months before we could go out west. It was time to get back to my crazy and beloved world of instructing teenagers. After all, according to some park rangers, I was one of them.

Chapter 2
(But It's a Dry Heat): Mid-June 2008

June. I remember being a kid and seeing JUNE as that great symbol of freedom-- a temporary release for good behavior. It often surprises people to learn that I absolutely hated school. I suppose I enjoyed kindergarten well enough, but then again, I didn't start until noon or so. First grade through college, however, I considered it to be a necessary evil to be endured until society recognized me as an adult.

Now, as a teacher, I stand on the other side of the line. I decide the workload, and I get *paid* to go to school. As it turns out, I do not hate school; I just want to be in the driver's seat. Nevertheless, even though I love my job, JUNE still looms as a prize.

I agreed to some extra cash via an easy summer school teaching assignment. It only went a few weeks, so by mid-June, I was free to pursue a brief glimpse of retirement. This, to me, was a strange concept. I understand working one job and getting paid. I understand working two jobs and getting paid. I do not understand working no jobs and getting paid. How bizarre. For the past eight months I had assumed I would get a summer job. Now, looking at the calendar, there were really only seven weeks available to work. After brief deliberation, I decided that it would be pointless to look for work for that short of time. Instead, I would go in the complete opposite direction. Rather than work and save money, I would loaf and spend reckless amounts of cash on my travel addiction. (If you're going to blow off responsibility, do it with flare.) The first order of business was the re-rescheduled Southwest trip.

Never one to mess around when vacation was involved, I determined we should leave the day after my last day of teaching summer school. Gear and clothes were packed, and the last-minute list lay on the kitchen table. It was vacation-eve, but there would be no traditional pizza. We had somehow psyched ourselves up to do a monodiet detox.

If you have no experience with a detoxification regimen, let me give you the pretty version. For a few days, you eat (or drink, on extreme programs) very cleanly, allowing your body to experience rejuvenation, deep anti-toxin cleansing, and overall euphoria. Desiring to start the summer off right and drop a few pounds along the way, we agreed to dedicate the first three days of our trip to the Apple Diet. Friday, Saturday, and Sunday, we would consume nothing but water and organic apples. I reasoned that this would work on physical, mental, and spiritual levels, as I envisioned communing with God's nature and returning to a simpler existence. After all, I had conquered the Master Cleanse just two months before. If I could live on lemonade for ten days, three days of apples should be a snap.

On day one, we drove to the car rental agency to pick up our covered wagon to head west. I have no love for rental cars, but since my truck was too small for our junk, and I still cannot drive Senator's manual transmission, it seemed the only option. We went into the office to fill out the necessary paperwork. "Will you be the only driver?" the man inquired.

"Yes." (*lie*)

"Do you want the basic or upgraded damage coverage?" (*sneaky, sneaky*)

"Wait a minute. I do not want any damage coverage. No extra anything. Just the car."

"Do you have rental car coverage on my auto insurance policy if something happens?"

"Yes." (*who knows?*) The agent showed us to the Chevy Cobalt that would be our companion for the next ten days. I smiled, thanked him, and Senator and I drove back to the house separately.

Until I am officially on the road, it is hard for me to exit worker bee mode. I rehearsed the mental list of what was going where in the car, and the very last minute things that had to be done. When we got home, we immediately began relaying sleeping bags, pillows, tent paraphernalia, clothes, food, maps, etc. out to the car. I was working at a pretty good pace, despite the drizzle, until I hit the small patch of unnoticed moss on the deck. Wham! Down the few stairs I went. That sucked. I could feel three distinct places of pain, but fortunately none were life-or-vacation-threatening. Feeling like an idiot, (especially when a few tears debated trickling,) I picked myself up and continued packing, at a slightly modified fervor.

At last we and everything we would need during the next ten days were tucked safely into the car. When you take a road trip beginning in Illinois, the first day's agenda is usually simple: drive the interstate as far as possible until the lines become blurry, or you find yourself in an ocean. (If the latter occurs, congratulations! You made great time!) In our case, we would take I-80 west through Iowa and into Nebraska. Most likely we would stop halfway through the state.

This worked through Illinois. Fifty miles into Iowa, however, the scenario changed drastically. State troopers diverted traffic to the exit ramp and completely shut the highway down, due to flooding. *That can happen?* I somehow subconsciously believed that interstates were magical roads, immune to the forces of nature. On the other hand, I couldn't say I was totally surprised, given our track record of heralding disasters to various cities (see my other travelogues).

The state police directed us to go back almost to the Illinois border and take a different highway north. Way north. Then we were supposed to follow it west. Way west. Finally we would come back south to rejoin I-80 in drier areas. This was the shortest possible route, but it would still add about 230 miles to our day. Thinking back, I had heard that Cedar Rapids had flooded the week before, but did not think much about it since it was thirty miles north of the interstate.

As it turned out, pretty much the entire state of Iowa was under water. In fact, some experts claimed that the state was sitting atop a 500-year flood plain, and this was apparently the 500th year. Really. What ace determined this? Are we basing this off of early Sixteenth Century drawings by the natives? Did the tribes who inhabited modern-day Iowa back in 1508 sketch out stick people and teepees floating away downstream? Or did the insurance companies hit upon the idea that a 500-year flood plain would not necessarily have to be covered under their current policies? I will let you decide.

For the next six hours, we tuned in to local radio, trying to keep up with the ever-changing flood detours. The station we found most useful (and entertaining) was hosted by a d.j. who had been evacuated from his station, and was now working with a folding table, chair, single telephone line, and prehistoric transmitter. Various people called in. Some offered helpful tips, like new road closings or help line phone numbers for people who were displaced.

Then there were the other callers. These dim individuals seized the opportunity to claim what they perceived to be their fifteen seconds of fame. They called to complain about drivers on the road (forgetting that they were drivers, too,) or to state the obvious. "Boy, it sure is a mess out there. I've never seen so much water. The levee really couldn't handle that much."

Thank you, Caller. The host was getting tired and irritated. He had passed the point of trying to hide his true feelings. After one particularly idiotic caller, he hung up and pronounced flatly, "That guy's gonna' die in this."

We stair-stepped our way through Iowa, chomping apples occasionally. It seemed that every time we were on a good run, we came to a road closure. Okay, I guess go west for a while. Road Closed. Try south then. Detour. Now west again. This went on for hours until we finally made our way back to the interstate. Iowa is a pretty, and very clean state, but I did not need to see that much of it. I was bound to make it into Nebraska.

We crossed the border and stopped at a rest area. Senator took over, with a second wind and renewed sense of purpose. Now we were going to drive, darn it. At some point in this gritty determinism, Senator chucked his last apple core out the window and opened a bag of cashews. I was not hungry, so the apples were sufficient. He drove until after 9:00pm, when the sun finally started to fall to the horizon. I always forget that, even within the same time zone, the sun sets at different times. We live on the very east edge of the Central Time Zone, so we lose daylight first, before the sun heads west to the rest of the zone. On the other hand, we get an earlier sunrise, so if you are one of those people who likes to be outside at 5:30am, you can conveniently see what you are doing. I am in no way, shape, or form one of those people.

We found an inexpensive hotel and checked in. Even with the flood detours, we had gone as far as originally hoped. We were conquerors. Rrraaaarrhhh! My growl of victory turned into a groan as I undressed and bumped my new bruise. The vague region between my right hip and butt cheek was colored an exquisite purply-blue. I ran my fingers over the spot, which had acquired a smooth texture. I tried to convince myself that it was nothing a few days of cleansing apples couldn't heal. Yeah, whatever. It was time to watch some mindless cable and drift off to sleep.*

Day two saw us out of bed early and on the road toward the West. The drive through the remainder of Nebraska seemed like a good time to start our book group. Sometimes we take a book that we can read together and discuss when we go on a road trip. This trip's selection was *The Island of Dr. Moreau* by H. G. Wells. Why I chose a sci-fi title set in the tropics for a trip to the mountains and desert, I do not recall. Nevertheless, the story began promisingly, with a old man retelling his strange story that began, as many strange stories do, with a shipwreck. Various loathsome characters soon entered the scenes. I read on as Senator drove into Colorado.

The scenery changed from corn to scraggly brush. There is not much to be seen in northwest Colorado, unless you are into the whole cowboy/ranch culture. I respect that they work hard, but I could do without having to gag my way past a slaughterhouse that reeked for miles. When the air cleared, I rummaged around for another apple. I was committed to this thing, but I was certainly not enjoying the light, clean, soothing feelings I had expected. Senator encouraged me to keep going, but he was no dummy. By now he was going wild with raw fruits *and* nuts. How very decadent.

Denver loomed on the horizon. We drove through it and wound our way through the improving scenery into the foothills of the Rockies. Here, we were amazed to see bicyclists on the interstate. It was enough of an effort to keep the car at a constant speed between the hills and curves. I cannot imagine trying to control a bike, especially knowing that you could get creamed by one of many passing vehicles at any moment.

---

*Who knew that Dame Judi Dench did Britcoms?

The Continental Divide came and went anticlimactically. I wondered what would happen if you stopped on the line and poured water on the ground. Would half go east and half go west? My thoughts were interrupted when a pebble from the truck in front of us smacked into the windshield. It left an impressive gouge, and I had visions of the rental agency sending me a bill for a new windshield. At least it was not spreading. In a twisted sort of way, it was actually pretty. The bright sun was reflecting off the leftover mounds of mountain snow, giving the chipped out portion a diamond-like gleam.

It was shortly after this that we stopped at the Greatest Rest Area Ever. Those who know me know that public restrooms and I do not generally get along. Either something malfunctions, or it is too crowded, or I am creeped out beyond the ability to perform. This particular rest area, however, was a downright pleasant experience.

Not only was it immaculate and well-maintained, but the scenery was phenomenal (once you were outside, I mean). The cool breezes brought fresh air down from the mountains, and bounced off the brilliant snow. Pine trees and small alpine flowers lined the trail around the outside of the parking lot. Everything just felt cleaner, no thanks to the stupid apples. In fact, it would have been a great place to share a pizza and other activities, had it not been so crowded.

Back on the road we consulted the general itinerary. We had planned to stay in western Colorado, but higher speed limits and the absence of cops for hundreds of miles shaved several hours off of the drive. We decided to drive on to Moab, Utah. Senator had fallen in love with Moab about eight years prior. He was instantly drawn to the small town culture set among the wild rugged rocks and the dry heat. In fact, the first time I ever heard of the town was when he mentioned it in a song he wrote for me before we were dating. The myth and curiosity had been growing in my mind ever since. Maybe in going there I would understand an even deeper part of him.

Under the late afternoon sun, we entered Moab. I was excited to finally be there, but Senator had a different impression. It seemed much had changed in eight years. The quiet, isolated refuge of independent desert dwellers had morphed into a tourist mecca for off-roaders and a fair amount of pseudo-naturalists. I think he was disappointed, if not heartbroken.

One thing that had not changed was the arid climate. Generally I like cooler weather and Senator likes warmer weather, but we are fierce allies against humidity. The wonderfully dry air was clocking in at about 10% humidity, which is perfect in our book. With no rain in the forecast, I was eager to get to a campground and set up the tent. I have always loved camping, and when the weather cooperates, it is a fun, inspiring experience, even when one is living on apples.

We paid our fee and drove to the site. It was not very big, but the views of the rust-colored mesas were stunning, and it was our home for the next two nights. I crawled in and set up the bed. 10% humidity notwithstanding, when you are crawling in a nylon tent and maneuvering floppy sleeping bags around on a summer evening in the desert, it is hot. Darn hot. I finished the bed and sucked on my water bottle. For the past few weeks I had been training my brain not to complain about the heat. As I kept my thoughts to myself, Senator vocalized his. "No. This is just too hot. We're never moving here."

What?! I was shocked. So now he understood. The boy who swore he would move to the desert the second I gave in now decided that summer was just too stinking hot there. I played it cool. "Oh?" I said casually, "Well, maybe when we are retired we can come down here for the month of February," I offered. I simultaneously felt relieved for myself and a little sad for him, but he seemed confident in his new revelation. I think we were both shocked. I think we both still are.

The evening was slipping away too fast to begin a hike, but there was time for a drive through Arches National Park. I do not recall seeing yellow stones at Yellowstone, but there are definitely arches at Arches. If you have ever seen a tourism ad for the state of Utah, chances are you have seen a photo from Arches National Park. Unusual and sometimes oddly balanced rocks are the result of erosion and changing underground salt beds. They are both formidable and fragile. The varied grooves and nooks give specific character to many of the formations. There are windows, whispering gossips, and a massive pipe organ for starters. As you get lost in the vista, your eyes and imagination will combine to find endless other images. It is not unlike finding colossal creatures in the clouds.

After many stops along the road for staged photo ops, we made our way out of the park. The rocks were casting longer and longer shadows until the entire park took on a new purple hue. I wondered if my bruise was disappearing yet. It was not in a place I thought often to check. Chomp. I took another bite of apple. I was beginning to hate apples. At least I was past the halfway point.

The desert was cooling off quickly and comfortably. In fact, it had dropped over 20°F from the time we arrived. We took a short walk around the campground. Fast lizards and bunnies darted all across the path. They were so tame that they did not move until they were about to be stepped on. I was later glad that I learned about the bunnies in the daylight. At night, all you could see was a large, dark lump in the road. It could have been any critter, given the right imagination. The moon was exceptionally bright, obscuring many of the stars, but still leaving far more than we see at home. I enjoyed the cool, dry night and drifted off, thankful that I had only one more apple day to go.

Sunday morning was warming up quickly. Riding high in his rejection of his apple diet, Senator opted for cooked food before going back to the national park. We stopped at the local hip organic café and he ordered an egg/veggie thing on a bagel. It came with tomato, which raised my eyebrow, as the Midwest had just experienced a salmonella scare with tomatoes. The girl at the register swore they were okay, and Senator was convinced they were fine, so he ate on. This is why we pray before meals. Thankfully, the tomatoes stayed put, and we left for Arches. Did I mention I now hated apples?

Our first objective once inside the park was the moderate to strenuous hike to Delicate Arch. Delicate Arch is the vertical rock formation that makes a giant hole, framing a portion of the red Utah desert. Chameleons and lizards scampered underfoot occasionally. I have a special affection for lizards and bats. Any animal that spends the majority of its life eating bugs that would otherwise seek me out as prey, is a friend indeed. The round trip was only three miles, but it seemed a little longer, since so much of it climbed and wound around.

At the top, I perched on what looked like the edge of a great bowl. I sat and drank more water, determining that I was now allowed to drink down to the halfway point of my supply. Across the rim was the arch, just like the August picture from my mom's national parks calendar. The sky was just as sapphire, too. It occurred to me that maybe nature photographers are not doing anything spectacular when they capture this scene; it can't help but be beautiful.

After poking around for a while, we started the walk back. It was only 9:00am, but the sun was getting vicious. I was hot and thankful that we were now on the descent. Mostly though, I was just amazed at the number of people hiking without any water. Are these people camels? Even the overweight and elderly were among the nonhydrated. This, I cannot understand. I am doing good if I take the garbage out without a water bottle. When I am working hard, I do not sparkle or glisten; I sweat. The only difference in the desert is that I sweat, it evaporates, and I sweat more. The end result is a multi-layered salty film. I took another swig as we arrived at the car. Now gimme a damn apple.

The next hike was one of those odd little jaunts that, though clearly drawn in on the trail map, never quite matches up to the map. To get to Broken Arch we had to drive into the campground, past the "Campers only beyond this point" sign, to a tiny, unmarked parking area. This was approximately where it *should* have been. The area was open enough that I figured I could find our way out, but something was still off. Ten minutes into the route, it forked. "I feel.... go right," I directed. Eventually we happened upon two great columns of rock.

"I think this is supposed to be Broken Arch," said Senator.

"That's funny. I never would have thought of two tall rocks in terms of a *potential* arch." There was nothing archlike about them, but I guess the park had an image to uphold. They reminded me more of a couple of lost members of Stonehenge. "Well, I guess you're right." The only problem was that, on the map, the arch was the end of the line, and this trail continued on, well out of sight. We followed it for another ten minutes, looked at each other, looked at the sun, and turned back in unanimous silence. We may or may not have seen Broken Arch, but we were satisfied.

Our last hike was a short walk to the Windows. The Windows are rock formations that really look more like a pair of hollow eyes. That is, unless the windows in your home happen to be horizontal ovals. The trail was short, with lots of steps. Go, thigh muscles, go. At the top was the payoff. The great arch provided shade for at least twenty people, and the breeze whipped through the opening like a giant fan. If I ever decide to take a tour of our nation's great napping spots, the Windows at Arches National Park will certainly be a stop. I'm getting sleepy just thinking about it...

We left the trails for the civilized air conditioning of the visitor center. It was small and standard, but anything I tried to read fell out of my brain. I do not function well mentally when I get hot. We gave up and entered the center's cool, dark theatre. Suddenly dozens of other tourists were also interested in the geological history of Utah. The screen zoomed through the eons, showing the cartoon rendition of the rise and fall of the local terrain. Storms crashed through the speakers and a legendary ocean swished. *I think I just found another great napping spot.* It was tempting to sit through a second round of the twenty-two minutes of air conditioned Discovery Channel bliss, but we were ready to move on.

Before leaving home, my neighbors had requested that we mail their five-year old son a post card. The truth is that there are not many children that I like. In fact, some days I have a hard time being around anyone else under the age of thirty. Eric is a special exception, though. He regularly visits me when I am out weeding gardens, even pulling a few weeds while talking. What other kindergartener knows the difference between periwinkle and dandelions? The week before leaving, he commented that he liked our new mulch. He also gives me regular weather reports (including tornado sightings), and never misses the opportunity to ask how my day went if he sees me pull up after work. He is not all business, though. Every so often he likes to see how far he can string me along. Take the day that he informed me that there were wild bears living on the outskirts of our town, for instance. Now that's a cool kid.

I bought a card and sat down to write. I realized that the last time I wrote to a five-year old, I probably was one. "Senator, what would you have wanted to read on your very own piece of mail when you were five?" We brainstormed, and then I began. I skipped the traditional small talk in favor of lizard descriptions and rock speak. Then I added what I hope will go down as the greatest post-card-addressed-to-a-five-year-old-boy line ever.

"We learned that the dinosaurs used to live here... but we did not see any today." Satisfied, we drove to a drug store to find a mailbox and drop off some film.

Back at the campsite, I was wilting. Senator was not in much better shape. We decided to go swimming, but it was crowded with people, bugs, and leaves. When we had killed enough time, we went back to the drug store to pick up the film. Of course, the one picture that I was looking forward to putting on my desk at school did not turn out. I chomped my apple hard.

Senator was getting hungry too, so he suggested we take scenic Route 128 to find a shady picnic spot by the Colorado River. It sounded perfect. Maybe we could read another dose of *Island of Dr. Moreau*. We drove back into the cliffs and mesas, but every pull off was in the blazing sun. We finally came across a lovely area, complete with shaded picnic tables, but it had a large sign declaring it a "U.S. Fee Area". What was that? You mean to tell me that our combined federal income taxes could not spot us fifteen minutes to make a stupid sandwich?

We prayed for shade, literally. I thought of the Sunday School stories about stoic prophets dying of thirst in the desert. I pictured the two-dimensional flannelgraph character (who was either Job or Ezekiel or Peter or Paul depending on need), sitting on his two-dimensional rock, staff in hand, praying for relief and wondering what idiot forgot to bring the map that could have saved them forty years' worth of wandering. I was getting loopy again. *Oh, man, do I need some shade.*

Just when I had almost given up, Senator spotted a shady pull off, complete with a breeze coming up from the water. The way the sun was moving, it guaranteed our shade for the remainder of the evening. For more than an hour and a half we read, relaxed, and visited like good friends. Now and then a fish jumped, or a duck floated down the river. The air was dry. Two or three times different cars pulled up and quickly left, perhaps afraid of what nefarious activities might prompt an out-of-state car and its two questionable inhabitants to sit for so long staring at rocks with all of the car doors open. When we judged the heat bearable, we drove back through town to our campsite.

With my brain back in functioning mode, I was able to win a few games of Battleship and concede multiple Yahtzee losses. On this trip, at least, I had an eerie ability to easily pinpoint the location of Senator's ships. I suppose I sort of have a strategy, but in reality, most people tend to scatter their plastic vessels in roughly the same patterns. There ought to be a way to make some cash off of this. Maybe I'll be the country's first Battleship hustler. We could work as a team. *Hi. This is my girlfriend, Wendy. She doesn't really know anything about military or psychological strategy, but she thinks the ships are adorable. Can she play you a game?*

We walked to the shower house and parted ways. All showers feel good, but some showers feel *earned*. This was one of them. I reveled in the night air that dried my hair in one hour, rather than the typical eight hours at home. Some days I consider chopping it all off, but then Senator threatens to do the same with his hair, which leaves us at a stalemate.

We sat quietly at the picnic table, watching the sky. Supposedly we were in the thick of a meteor shower, but the moon was so bright it was hard to tell. I reflected on the day. My legs felt tight, but good. I did not particularly feel healthier, but I had survived three days of apples, and I was looking forward to the change in menu.

With that, I looked up and saw, directly over Senator's head, the largest meteor flash that I had ever witnessed. Whereas a common meteor shower has many flashes of white pinpoint light that disappear as soon as you realize they are there, this was another experience altogether. A green glow that appeared to be size of my hand flashed brilliantly, and took at least ten full seconds to fade. My jaw dropped. Professional fireworks could not be so stunning. This brief moment would have been enough to make the trip worthwhile. Convinced nothing could top that spectacle, we crawled into the tent and slowly dozed off.

It is rarely pleasant to wake up at 4:00am when you are sleeping in a tent. It means one of two things: 1.) you are awake for no reason, but there is nothing to do but lay there and be bored until your significant other or the sun arises, or 2.) something is wrong, very wrong. As I tossed and kicked covers off, I knew something was wrong. There was a vague feeling that I recognized, but could not place within my half-dormant fog. My heart was racing, but I felt very weak at the same time. Water. I needed water. No, I think I know this feeling. I was about to throw up. I struggled to get my clothes and shoes on, telling Senator I would be back shortly. I stumbled my way the half-block to the bathrooms. I was so weak that it was more exhausting than all of the previous day's hikes. *Please, God. Not here.* I had not been sick in years. Why now, on vacation?

I locked myself inside a roomy, plywood stall. Thankfully, there was a sink, too. I crouched down in that awkward position between not touching anything for sanitary reasons, and wanting to collapse on the floor. Nothing happened, but the feeling would not leave. I stood up to regroup. I had reached a point of commitment. I just wanted it over with so I could go back to sleep. *Three days of living on organic apples, and this is how my body thanks me!*

Just then I heard a knock at the door. "I brought you oranges..." Generally people do not think to offer a nauseous person oranges, but Senator was convinced I was wilting from hunger, and he knew that oranges are always the first food the digestive system can handle after a fast or monodiet. I smiled weakly. I felt bad that I woke him up, but I was also glad he was there.

"Thanks, Baby, but I can't. Could you maybe just bring me my toothbrush?" I mumbled. Maybe it was a mental block and nothing was happening because I was so disgusted by the germs. I had to change the scene to something more conducive to my needs. Grabbing a huge wad of paper towels, I ran them under water and added a healthy amount of liquid soap. Looking up, I caught my ghostly reflection in the mirror. At least I looked pale and thin. Careful not to touch anything, I squeezed the towels out over the toilet rim, making sure to soak every inch in hot soapy water. I crouched down again. *Okay....now!* I tried to will myself to get sick, but still nothing happened. I changed my prayer. *Okay, God. The toilet is clean. It's 4:30am, in a campground in the desert in Utah. If I'm going to puke, make it happen in the next five minutes, or I am refusing to be sick and going back to bed. Amen.*

Soon there was another knock at the door. "Are you alright? I've got your toothbrush."

"I'll be out in a minute. Well, actually about three more minutes." Nothing happened and time ran out, so I unlocked the door, leaving puddles of institutional-smelling soapy water in my wake. "I'm ready to go back now."

The ordeal had weakened me even more. I leaned on Senator for the entire walk back. When we reached the campsite, the dawn was just breaking. We sat on the picnic table and I sipped water. Senator mounted his campaign to make me eat the oranges. "Okay, I think I can try one." I sat like a lump while he hand-fed me tiny morsels of orange, as if I was a baby bird. Slowly I managed to get almost half an orange down. When I was certain it was staying down, I went back to bed. Senator joined me and we were out instantly.

A few hours later we woke up. I could not believe the difference. I felt rested, refreshed, and ready to take on the day. It was as if the previous event was a dream. I was even excited when I realized that today was the day I could EAT. The moral of the story is: never detox on vacation. Though I knew this rule, I believed that it would be okay since I was not actually fasting. Stupid, stupid, stupid.

Monday morning, take two. We were now gladly on our way to Zion National Park, on the other side of Utah. We faced several hours of scarcely-populated interstate and surprisingly varied terrain. The stretch of I-70 that crosses Utah is gorgeous. We saw rock in most of the colors of the rainbow, and wove in and out of lush national forest. Some areas were cool and breezy, and others left no mistake that it was summer. Majestic mesas eventually gave way to rolling hills, and then back to towering rock formations.

A little after noon we arrived in Springdale, the town directly outside of the park's entrance. It was crowded and hot, but attractive, and full of flowers. We tuned the radio to the looped tourist information. The automated voice (that I think every national park uses) told us that no cars could drive through the park. We would have to take a shuttle because it was too crowded. At the entrance a ranger was directing traffic to park a block away, on some blacktop. We were unprepared for this. We wanted to hike three different trails, and return to the car in between each one to refill water bottles, check the map, etc. Now we had to think of everything we would need for the entire afternoon. We gathered our junk and crossed the pavement, which served as its own little radiating inferno.

Moments later the shuttle pulled up, and we were herded onto the non-air conditioned bus. It might have helped if the windows opened all the way, but I guess they figured someone like me would lean my head all the way out and probably get struck by the outbound shuttle. At the first trailhead, we disembarked and began the walk, which, thankfully, culminated in a shaded waterfall pool. A man was playing a flute in the hollow, surrounded by red rock and green forest plants. This was lovely, but we wanted to see more of the park, and it certainly was not getting any cooler.

We hopped the shuttle again, and opted for another hike to a waterfall, appropriately named Weeping Rock. Either you made it to where the rock seeped steadily, or you cried trying. Smaller streams trickled down the cliffs. The cold, clear liquid looked inviting, but given my morning's start, I did not want to take my chances with foreign microbial enemies. At the end of the trail we sat on the clammy rocks, looking out from behind the thin waterfall. I could see why the Mormons named this place Zion. It was truly beautiful.

We viewed the rest of the park from the bus. It was not ideal, but it was more than we would have seen on foot. Occasionally the driver would point out interesting facts or other trails. Indicating a cliff about 1,400 feet up, he explained that there was a rim trail there. He advised that no one who was afraid of heights attempt it, though. In one part the trail was only three feet wide, with sheer drop-offs on either side. "But it's okay," he said, "There are chains to hold on to." No thanks. Not today, anyway. In fact, it had already reached 101°F instead of the predicted 89°F.

We ended our day in Zion National Park and drove toward our reserved campsite. The complex included a hotel, RV park, and campground. Senator needed to eat and replenish his salt, so I went in alone to register. The man behind the counter gave me a site map and the requisite windshield card. Then he told me that there was also a $3.00 tax. Fine, whatever. He handed me my receipt and two small metal pieces. He explained that they were necessary to work the showers. We were each sweaty and anxious for a shower now, and I knew if we went swimming we would want one in the morning, too. "Is it possible to get more?" I asked.

"Sure. They're $5.00 each, and they go for six minutes."

Now I was annoyed. After all, twenty-five bucks a night to tent camp was nothing to sneeze at. They could at least provide a decent shower. There was nothing else available in town. Throughout our conversation several people without reservations had been turned away, so there was not much I could do. I used my only recourse. "Boy, you guys just get us coming and going, don't you?"

I returned to the car and explained the shower situation to Senator. We then drove the loop to find our spot. RVs and tents were crammed everywhere. "Our spot should be coming up," I ventured. Then I saw it. Imagine a gravel driveway that is slightly wider than a mall parking space, and *almost* twice as long as a compact car. That was what qualified as a tent site. To make matters worse, on one side of us was an RV with a loud generator running, and on the other side were the Ja-fake-ans. These fat, white morons were cranking Bob Marley and smoking a few to enhance their outdoor experience.

The ensuing family meeting was inevitable. We perched on rocks by the shores of a creek that would have been scenic if it were anywhere but here. That we both wanted to leave immediately was agreed. That we would be able to find somewhere else to stay was a debatable point. I had flashbacks of the miserable night we spent four years before, driving through the drunken party that was Jackson Hole, Wyoming, until 2:00am, when we finally found available lodging. Here, if we could not find anywhere to stay, it would mean driving hours to the desolate North Rim of the Grand Canyon. We would then have to spend the night in the car, parked and waiting for the main gate to open.

All I wanted was a shower and the opportunity to cook real food for the first time since leaving home. The more I thought about it, the angrier I became. Senator had been building his case, but he need not continue. "Come on. Let's get the heck out of here! And mark my words: I *will* get my money back!" Hell hath no fury like that of a hot, hungry, tired camper woman scorned.

I could feel my eyes growing greener. This time Senator went into the office with me, but as it turned out, I handled it pretty well by myself. "We are not going to stay here and I need my money refunded," I announced in a single breath. The desk clerk refunded the $3.00 tax. "No. I want the entire $28.00 back," I explained, eyes glowing more verdantly.

"Oh. I can't do that, Miss."

"Then you need to find the manager who can." The manager popped in, eating potato salad out of a carton. "What's the problem?" he asked casually, between gloppy bites.

"The problem is that we are not going to stay here and I need my money refunded. Your sites are the worst excuse for tent sites I have ever seen! Your website *grossly* misrepresents the gravel parking lot you call a campground. Then you have the nerve to limit and charge extra for showers. Now here is my credit card. I need the money refunded. In full." (Never piss off a writer. We are seldom at a lost for words.)

"Okay, I'll put it back on right now," he agreed.

I was shocked. I did not even need to crack open the second round of ammunition. "Okay. Thank you for handling this. I'll just need a receipt."

"It won't print out a receipt, but I'll go refund it right now. You can come watch me if you want to." He had a dab of potato salad on the side of his lip.

I thought fast. "Well, I'm being reimbursed for this, so I need a receipt showing the credit." (*lie*) He then instructed the desk clerk to sign the slip saying that it would be refunded. I thanked him curtly and we left. I had clearly won that battle, forcing the opponents to resort to a give-this-broad-her-money-so-she'll-get-out surrender. After I calmed down, and reveled in Senator's victorious and approving grin, I shifted uncomfortably as I pondered the task ahead. This night was either going to get much better, or much worse.

We determined we had better stop for gas as soon as possible since we had no idea how long we would be driving. Though the Grand Canyon was only a few hours away, there were only four towns between the two points, and they were four towns that could have combined and still not equaled a city. Senator pumped gas while I went in to use the bathroom. For the second time in less than twenty-four hours, I prayed in the stall of a public restroom. *Okay, God. Yeah, me again. Thanks, by the way, for the not-puking, and thanks for the oranges and for my guy who brought them to me. So it turns out we are homeless for the night, but I'm going to choose to believe that you have something better up your sleeve. After all, that is how you've always worked in my life, so why should this be any different, right? Amen.* I exited the bathroom and hopped back in the car. "I think we made the right decision," I told Senator. He nodded.

We drove down the country route, past a few cows and many fields. Just two miles down the road we passed by an unadorned iron sign that read, "Rocky Top B&B-- vacancy". It sounded too good to be true. "Should we stop?" asked Senator. I reasoned that we could always take a look, and if it was bad, we could keep driving. We had nothing to lose, so we pulled into the long driveway. It was not one of the fancy bed and breakfasts that you see in the full color, tri-fold brochures. In fact, it looked quite lived-in, and the porch made no pretense of being cleaned up for company. We were a little wary.

Before we could get out of the car, a 20ish red-headed western girl bounded out of the house. She greeted us cheerfully, but we wanted information before committing to anything. "What can you tell us about your rooms?" Senator asked her.

"Well, it's really only one room, but it's more like an apartment. There's no breakfast, though, because we don't have much food in the house today." That seemed odd, but breakfast was the least of our concerns. "I can show you the place if you like. It's out back over my grandparents' garage. This is their place. I just stay here for the summer because it's cooler." *Cooler than where?* we wondered, remembering the soaring mercury of the afternoon.

"I'm from Las Vegas," she explained as she unlocked the door to the apartment. Inside was an immaculate and tastefully decorated suite, complete with full kitchen and linens. I quickly scanned the rooms for clues as to the legitimacy of the business. In the bathroom was a homemade copy of a book called *Clean Jokes of My Friends and Family*. On the kitchen counter lay a guest book, signed by a couple from Germany who had fallen in love with the charming apartment. That was good enough for me. Now I wondered if we could afford it. When she told us the price, though, I almost laughed. A place like that would easily be twice as much in the Midwest. We eagerly told her we would take it.

The three of us walked back to where we had parked, and we naturally started to follow her back to the porch. "Oh," she said once she realized we were expecting paperwork, "You don't have to fill anything out. You can just pay me." It sounded a little fishy, but we had seen the clean shower and bed, and nothing was going to stand in our way.

As we climbed the stairs to our new paradise, Senator joked, "How long do you think it will be until the cops come and raid the place?"

"As long as it is after I get a shower, I don't care!" We cleaned up and then enjoyed the bonus of a kitchen-cooked meal. Because I am never content to cook simply, I indulged in a mess that resulted in fried potatoes and onions, along with vegetable-cheese omelets. We were clean and full. *Wow. Good going, God.* After an unscored game of Scrabble (also provided by our invisible grandparent-hosts) we crawled into bed. Again, the moon was intensely bright, and it had cooled to a suitable temperature for window opening. New York's finest hotels had nothing on these accommodations.

The next morning we woke up lazily, as the sun streamed across the yard. We were half tempted to cancel our itinerary and park ourselves here for another five days, but there was much more to see. One of the great things about being a realist is that you are never disappointed by how much you have to spend. When it comes to money, you are either on target, or you walk away with a little extra. When it comes to time, you over plan, and end up with more leisure hours.

While I had somehow calculated another four hours to get to our next stop, it only took about two and a half hours. This was especially useful since we would lose an hour crossing into Arizona. Though it is still in the Mountain Time Zone, the state does not bother with the hassle of daylight savings time, much to their credit. One time schedule, consistently and forever.

We left our cozy b&b, and I braced myself for the intense heat that I always associated with the Grand Canyon. The last time I had been there was when I was fifteen, and I remember the searing sun. That was at the South Rim, though. This trip we were going to the North Rim, where neither of us had ever ventured.

After driving a while, we stopped for gas and some fruit. *Best to eat light and stay cool*, I thought as we drove south through canyon country wilderness. When we entered Arizona, we had a pleasant surprise. We found ourselves amid thick rolling pine and aspen trees in the Kaibab National Forest. The sun was strong, as expected, but the temperature kept dropping every few miles. It was now in the mid 70s, according to the car's thermometer. We rolled down the windows to test it for ourselves. Sure enough, a dry cool breeze flew through the car. This was not the Arizona we knew.

After winding through the forest, we came to a large open meadow, with deer feeding in the distance. If I were blindfolded and dropped off here, I would have guessed I was in the Rocky Mountains of northern Colorado, or even Minnesota. When we drove up to the ranger's station at the entrance, I checked the posted forecast, convinced that this must be some fluke. I was glad to be wrong when I learned that this was average June weather here. This, I could do.

It was too early to set up camp, so we wasted no time driving to the first trailhead. The North Rim is situated in a such a way that it would be a peninsula if it was surrounded by water. The long, narrow strip of land points south toward the other side of the canyon, but with even more spectacular views, as it rises another 2,000 feet over the South Rim. The Cape Royal trail was an easy, paved walk that took us out to one edge. The colorful layers of rock surrounded us on three sides. In the far distance to the east, the land looked like a giant, light green table. I will not even attempt to describe the beauty accurately, because it is far too awesome. Just know that, if you have never been there, it is every bit as breathtaking as the best footage you have seen. Make it a point to go to the Grand Canyon, and if you have to choose, go to the North Rim.

Another benefit of going to the North Rim rather than the South Rim (beside the fact that there are only 10% as many tourists) is the variety of trails. Our second hike took us into a completely different landscape. The Cliff Springs trail began by going down into a rocky forest, and was eventually flanked by smaller canyons and a running stream. It actually resembled the Illinois River Valley region at home. Yet another walk, to Point Imperial, was surrounded by small brush and grasses. This hike resulted in a unique view of the Painted Desert, as well as the land to the northeast of the Grand Canyon.

It was now time to check into our campsite. I had made the reservation for two nights, and even chosen online what seemed like a good site. Given the previous night's experience, however, I was somewhat cautious. The friendly lady at the booth gave us our information and off we went. When we pulled up to our assigned spot, I was relieved. Here, at a cheaper rate than the horrible place we left the night before, was a vast, shady spot that could have easily accommodated seven tents. Pine needles covered the ground, and the temperature was perfect, despite the late afternoon sun.

Once we were unpacked, we were ready to reward ourselves with showers. The pay showers, we were told, took six quarters for seven minutes. It was not ideal, but it was better than $5.00 for six minutes. This would be a new venture for me. We walked up to the shower house. I was hoping for 'family bathrooms', where you could maximize your time and privacy, but instead there were separate men's and women's sides.

Senator walked in the men's room and waited for someone to finish so he could go in. I walked into the women's and waited in the steamy, sweaty, dirty line of eight. This was a fiasco in itself. There were six showers, but one was reserved for handicapped campers (which I respect, though I have never seen anyone use one), and one was broken. Of the remaining four, one was inhabited by a slow woman, and two others were being shared by a mother and daughter who could not understand the coin machine, despite our group efforts to teach them. I seriously considered walking into the men's bathroom and using one of their showers. After all, every stall had locking doors.

The line inched forward as two girls stepped out. I surveyed the situation. There was a lesbian couple in front of me. *Good. Hopefully they'll go in together and only take up one.* No such luck. I waited another ten minutes until there was an opening.

I sprinted in and began to plot. There was only one hook on the door (poor planning), so I would hang my bag there, but not take the towel out, in case it fell to the filthy wet floor below.

I lined up my quarters in the machine without pushing them in yet. I lay another set of spares next to them, in case I was cut off mid-shampoo. I knew I did not generally take long showers, but did I usually average over seven minutes? Who knows?

When everything was ready, and I had rehearsed the steps in my mind, I hopped in, released my coins, and was almost nailed against the back wall by the water pressure. I sped through my routine, wishing there was a count-down clock so I could gauge my progress. When I had rinsed the last of the conditioner out of my hair, I tried to the turn the water off, but there was no way to do so. I stood there like an idiot, feeling a little guilty for wasting water. At least I knew I could beat the clock. I casually planned dinner in my head as I held up each finger to power wash the dirt from under my nails. Just after number ten, the water abruptly stopped. I quickly dressed and left the bathhouse.

Upon returning to the campsite, we fired up the ol' Coleman for gourmet portobella reuben sandwiches and braised green beans. No hot dogs and chips here. Have olive oil, will travel. With our bellies full and reveling in the curiosity of the other campers, we cleaned up and drove to the lodge for the evening program.

There was plenty of time before the lecture, so we bummed around and watched the sun begin its descent. The cultural divide between the 'lodge people' and the campers was its own grand canyon. We campers were in jeans and dirty shoes that had been on trails all day. We carried flashlights and mused at how cold it would get that night. The lodgers were in creased pants, tucked in polo shirts, and even belts. They carried cocktails-- yes, I actually overheard this-- and fretted over when to make the next night's dinner reservations. As the sun sank below the high horizon, we watched the rainbow of changing color on the opposite canyon walls, amazed. They missed nature's show completely, and commented disappointedly that you could not see the sun go down all the way. *Sigh.*

The resident geologist put his entire twenty-one years of life experience into the evening presentation. The slide show corresponded with his lecture on creatures that swam around in the area when it was an ocean. Some were giant, toothy sharklike beasts, and others were minute, dumb-looking blobs. I recognized a few of the fossil illustrations from my science textbooks. I often wonder if the artists ever get feisty and take a little too much creative liberty. I pictured the scientist presenting the straight facts, and assigning the illustrator to make up the rest. "Really? You think he had blue hair and spotted tentacles?..."

We bid farewell to the other half and drove back to the campground. Our humble and comfortable bed beckoned us to regenerate for more hiking the next day. Before turning in, I took one more peak at the moonbeam. I never cease to be entranced by a brightly lit moon. It is like the well kept secret that sun worshipers miss out on. Too bad for them.

As I said before, a major advantage of the North Rim is the variety of trails. Wednesday morning Senator woke up first and stepped out of the tent. As the door flapped, I could feel that it was quite a bit cooler than the night before. He told me that he checked and it was only 60°F, but it would be getting warmer soon. We quickly got ready and drove to the Widforss trailhead.

This trail wound its way around a meadow and through the woods, climbing slightly. Just about the time you forgot where you were, glimpses of the Grand Canyon would peek between the trees at the edge. The best part may have been that the trail was empty and quiet. It was a perfect morning starter. We enjoyed it for several miles and returned to the car, where Senator made his confession. "I guess I can tell you now," he admitted. "It was actually only 40°F when you woke up." Hhmmm. That explained why I did not break a sweat.

For the next trail, we had to drive to the lodge parking lot. The Transept Trail took us along yet another view, looking out from the west side of the plateau. At the other end of the trail was a campground, where we could only shake our heads at what we saw. "Rented Excursions" was written on a white van that had twelve bicycles on top. The name said it all. Nearby, two men worked to spread picnic tables with tablecloths. Disturbingly clean coolers were positioned all around. We imagined the type of people who might attend such a charade. I watched the men from a distance, expecting them to unpack the Grey Poupon at any moment. What a joke. I wondered if they sold rented memories to those who attended the rented excursion.

Since the car was parked near the lodge, we made a pit stop in the visitor center. For such a great park, the visitor center was rather lame. It contained a few small displays, and many more noisy lodgers and their yuppies-in-training children. That was enough for me. It was time for lunch anyway.

Back at the campsite, we feasted on fried potatoes, onions, and toast with jam. Afterward we hit the road for a scenic drive. When we wanted to park and enjoy the view, we took turns reading our book, until we both fell asleep. The book was exciting, but so was the prospect of a breezy nap in the woods.

By now it was time to battle the coin showers once more. I had firmly made up my mind to go to the guy's bathhouse if the line was as bad as the day before. I figured that I could be showered and gone by the time anyone official came to kick me out. Senator and I parted ways and I checked the women's bathhouse. No one was in line. Seizing the opportunity, I ducked in a stall. The water of that shower was running, so I prepared my stuff and got my coins ready for when it ran out. I stepped in and took my shower, expecting at any minute to have the water shut off. It did eventually shut off, less than five seconds after I finished. Woo-hoo! Free shower for me! Take that! I emerged victorious, excited to tell Senator.

When dinner time rolled around, I was ready to create my final camp stove meal of the vacation. Together we diced and sauteed and sliced the ingredients for hearty burritos. "To the North Rim," we toasted, holding up the leaking wraps. God bless Mr. Coleman.

The final event of the evening was an outdoor ranger program. Our lecturer began by opening the floor for any questions that anyone might have during the program. It was a casual atmosphere, and she told fun tales. A few moments into one story, a little boy raised his hand and asked a question. Patiently, she answered, as everyone smiled on politely. She continued, but was interrupted shortly thereafter by another kid question. The audience's attention began to wander, as she tried to decipher what the child was asking. Of course, no parents intervened to help her.

When it happened a third time, no one even tried to feign interest. Everyone began their own hushed conversations as they ignored the uncomfortable dialogue between ranger and kid. So here, Reader, I implore you: know when a kid should be encouraged to partake in the adult world, and when he should be subtly told to cool it. The truth is, none of the rest of us are impressed with your kid's dumb question, and the ranger is most likely faking an answer anyway.[*]

When the stories came to an end, we thanked the relieved park ranger and walked back to our site. It was the perfect night for a fire, and the previous squatters had left wood in our fire pit. Senator fumbled around with matches and kindling, making fire

---

[*]As long as I am ranting, and I happen to be a former server, ditto for letting kids order in restaurants. No one thinks it is cute, and our time is far more precious than your kid's mispronunciation of the word 'manicotti'. By all means, play restaurant at home to teach him, but leave it there until he is at least sixteen. Agreed?

for us. We gazed at it silently for a long while. Somewhere in the sky there should have been a full moon, but so far I had not seen it.

As the embers burned down, we got ready for bed and then walked toward the tent. All at once, perched in a small gap of pine trees, the moonlight streamed through to the side of the tent. I was speechless. The sky had been alive all week, and this was the culmination. I had never seen such a bright full moon in my life, including those in winter that were reflected on the snow. I stared for a long time before going to bed. Then I looked out once more, just as it slid behind the trees.

The next day we left the North Rim bright and early. It was the day that I was least looking forward to. The only objective was to drive, drive, drive, until we could conquer no more. Again the temperature struggled to stay above 40°F, but that changed soon enough. After just one hour of descending from the Kaibab Plateau, the temperature was in the 70s. An hour later, it was in the 90s. The trees were long gone, now replaced by miles of barren, red dust.

Several times our route took us into or alongside the reservations[*]. One thing that seemed odd, however, were the roofs on many houses. They were covered in old tires. A roof might have twenty different tires lined up in rows. I suppose it might have had something to do with deflecting the heat from the tin. On the other had, it is hard to see how black rubber could have anything to do with cooling something. Here, I invite your well-researched answers.

As I said, we were back in the real Arizona. No more cool breezes or shady pullovers. Even in an air conditioned car

---

[*]For what it is worth, the reservations did not appear as poverty stricken as I remembered. Maybe things were improving somewhat. Wouldn't that be a fascinating irony? Imagine if, just as the white man's economy was in a severe downturn, the native standard of living was rising.

we drank our water bottles quickly. This was not a problem as we carried a gallon water jug in the back seat at all times. Not wanting to waste time pulling over, I squirmed in and out of my seat belt to reach the jug. With my entire 5'1" frame stretched from the passenger's front seat to the driver side back seat, I lifted the jug from its spot on the floor. Carefully I hoisted it up, bumping the door slightly.

In an instant water was gushing everywhere. My first thought was to tighten the cap in annoyance at whomever had left it loose (probably me), but it was already tightened. It was one of those moments when everything moves in slow motion and you have several simultaneous thoughts: Thought #1: *My, this is strange. The fill hole is clearly sealed, and yet water is gushing about.* Thought #2: *I wonder how much water has spilled out already. If I could locate the source, perhaps I could plug it.* Thought #3: *I wonder what else got soaked.* Thought #4: *I better have this sucker dried out before it stains or molds. Here comes a damage bill from the rental car company.* Thought #5: *I should probably make an attempt to explain what's going on to Senator. He's spending too much time glancing toward the back seat instead of watching the road.* Thought #6: *Oh, crap!*

It was then that I realized that the minor bump into the door had hit the plastic just right to shatter a two-inch section of the corner. The floor and part of the seat were soaked, but I was more upset about the loss of my $2.00 water jug. It was the perfect size and shape for travel-- one of those love-at-first-sight purchases. Naturally, we had to pull over anyway, thereby rubbing salty irony into my wound. Fortunately, we managed to salvage most of the water and position the jug inside the cooler for the remainder of the trip. At least I got my drink of water.

I thought the rest of Arizona was desolate, until we entered New Mexico. I suppose it was attractive in a "Where shall we land our spacecraft once we reach that silly little planet called Earth?" sort of way. Mainly the billboards stand out in my mind, though. Every other one threatened drunk drivers. One promised that, "They *will* find you!" Another admonished drivers, "Don't even *think* about it." Hhmmm. I don't know about that one. I tend to believe that drunk drivers do enough 'not thinking about it'. In any case, call a cab if you plan to booze in New Mexico.

As we neared the Texas border, the humidity increased and we could see storms kicking up in the distance. It is true what they say. Everything in Texas is bigger. We watched the storm in the distance for about two hours before driving into it. The rain started slowly, but the wind picked up quickly. Then the rain took the cue and fell in sheets. Halfway through the pan handle, we decided to call it quits for the night. Thankfully, we had not planned to camp, so there was no disappointment there.

Instead, we found a reasonable motel and went in to get a room. I proudly presented my union card that, for the small sum of $600 per year in dues, was supposed to get me a 10% discount. "Don't know nothin' about it," the twenty-something behind the desk answered flatly. He was staring through me to the television across the room. He recited the basic information about the check-out time, where to park, and how to find the room. Then, in a moment of salesmanship, he offered, "Your room key gets ya' 15% off at the Mexican place over there." He vaguely gestured down the street.

That sounded good. We had been anticipating Tex-Mex food for a few days. "Oh? How's their food?" asked Senator.

Desk Boy shrugged. "I guess it's okay." Wow, what a ringing endorsement. We thanked him and did our best to dodge the rain as we grabbed our bags and ran outside to our room.

It was getting late, and soon the only Mexican restaurant that was open late enough was the room key discount place. Oh, what the heck. We drove less than a mile in the pouring rain and arrived at Ruby Margarita's. The hostess sat us and we chatted as we looked over the menu.

We waited for our server. Our menus were suggestively closed and hanging over the edge of the table. We looked around, but still no one came. Finally a dorky white kid showed up and apologized, explaining the whole background saga of who was supposed to pick up our table and why she didn't. *Yeah, yeah, yeah. Let's make with the enchiladas already.*

When our meals arrived, Senator's side order was incorrect. Hungry, tired, and anxious to get to a warm bed, we ate quickly. The server tried hard to sell us dessert, but we we just wanted our bill. I presented our room key for the discount. "Oh," the waiter feigned sympathy, "I wish you had shown me that before. I don't know if I can accept that." He tilted his head and made puppy dog eyes.

I made hunting dog eyes. Alright. That's enough. "Would you do me a favor and send your manager over, please?" While this was no crappy campground incident, as a former server, I could not let it go.

When the manager arrived, I calmly explained about the long wait, the wrong order, and the discount issue. For good measure I threw in the fact that the hotel was sending them business, and they should live up to that favor. I tactfully chose, however, to leave out the fact that we had better Mexican food in northern Illinois than he was serving. In fact, he was generally shocked that we did not think this was the greatest eatery ever. To his credit, he handled it well.

The server even came out of the deal with a generous tip, mainly because we could tell it was his first job, and I will always have a soft spot for a good-hearted teenager. It serves us right for not heeding the words of the wise desk clerk. Back at our room, deep sleep was the highlight of the day.

Friday morning was more promising. The storms had passed, and now large fair weather clouds loomed over the endless farmlands between us and my sister's home in Springfield, Missouri. We soon bid a fond farewell to Texas and entered Oklahoma. Oklahoma was picture perfect and unassuming. *Wow. This looks nothing like The Grapes of Wrath.* Somehow, when I pictured Oklahoma, it had not occurred to me that it might have recovered from the drought and dust storms that swept through the area over seventy years ago. Duh. The grass was deep green and the sky was deep blue and that was about it. Nothing else was necessary.

    Do not assume that Oklahoma is naive or timid, though. In fact, they have a pretty sly tollway system. When you get on I-44, you pay the turnpike fee immediately. At first this seems strange because everyone pays the same amount, though they are each traveling different distances. We were familiar with the turnpikes in the East, which charged you once you exited, and prorated the cost according to how far you drove on the road. Oklahoma plays it smart. They charge you the full amount up front. If you exit before the toll portion ends, you may present your recent for a refund of the difference. If you figure in the percentage of drivers who throw out, misplace, or give their receipt to their toddler to scribble on, the state comes out well ahead. I am not surprised that a state has invented this crafty system; I am just shocked that it was not Illinois. Maybe that is why they call it the Sooner State. The sooner you exit, the better off you are!

    When I initially mapped out our tentative route for this trip, I stood back and looked at the pencil outline on the U.S. map. Unintentionally, I had formed a giant loop that encircled the state of Kansas. Knowing that Kansas would never be a destination that we traveled to on purpose, I decided we had better at least jog through a corner of it. Otherwise, we might never be able to cross it off our list. With this in mind, we took a brief detour into the very southeast corner of Kansas before going into Missouri.

I can't say the scenery changed much. We saw more farms, more cows, and a few small towns scattered in between. It was while going through one of those villages, though, that we witnessed another stereotypical Kansas scene. On the left side of the street were old homes and buildings that stood quietly as they had for decades. On the right side, however, lay the remains of what was previously a small neighborhood. The mass scale demolition and twisted trees were the eerie and distinct calling card of a tornado that had recently gone through. It was not the first time I had seen tornado wreckage, but it is never any less dramatic. If you do not live in the middle of the country, it is hard to describe the sheer force that unbalanced pressure can have. *The Wizard of Oz* was set in Kansas for a reason. It only took traveling in the state for ten miles to see evidence of the natural disasters for which they are infamous.

Soon we crossed into western Missouri, land of the moronic drivers. After dodging and employing all the defensive driving strategies we knew, we arrived in Springfield. Springfield has much to offer as a city. Its best attraction in the summer of 2008 was its $3.67 gallon of gas. I won't tell you how much a gallon of gas cost when I started driving, but suffice it to say that no station needed three digits on its sign.

We pulled up to my sister's apartment and exchanged enthusiastic greetings. She gave us the latest tour of her home, and then we set about the serious business of deciding which pizza place to try. This is no small task in a college town. Eventually we settled on a Kansas-based chain that specialized in wheat crust and fresh toppings.

Wheat State Pizza was a real treat. For some reason, northern Illinois is sluggish when it comes to the whole wheat revolution as it pertains to pizza. Maybe they think they are betraying a great Chicago tradition by changing the crust. In reality, I'm sure wheat was used long before white flour, but who am I to take on the pizza establishment? I might end up in the

Chicago River wearing cement shoes, my mouth stuffed with wheat. No thank you.

After dinner we headed downtown. Springfield's downtown area is in the middle of a resurgence with positive results. There is a thriving art and photography community, and several galleries are available for browsing. In the summer months, regular art walks are scheduled to showcase local talent. Likewise, the city supports a budding live music scene, sometimes right within their local parks.

Then there is the coffee. In the several square blocks that make up the heart of the city, no less than ten independent cafés teem with caffeinated patrons on a weekend night. The lounges and night clubs were hopping the night we were there, too. What fascinates me most about the entertainment options in Springfield is that they exist in a relatively small city. At just over 150,000 people, Springfield easily competes with cities with half a million residents. Heidi explained that it is because Springfield is isolated. Once you leave the city limits, it is a quite a while before you come to anything that resembles a city. Suburbs are nonexistent.

In addition to the described amusements, Heidi also led us to a particularly unique view of historical Springfield. By the soft glow of the streetlights, we climbed stairs to a 100+ year old foot bridge. Then we listened for the familiar rumble. The bridge is positioned over a dozen or so operating train tracks. Nothing quite replicates the experience of a gleaming train headlight coming right at you as the smell of coal dust fills your nostrils, and your ears ring from the persistent whistle blast. The thrill reaches its peak when the train clamors beneath your feet, rattling the bridge just enough to make you wonder how many more good years are left in it.

The bridge stopped vibrating and we stepped our way down to street level. We returned to the car, which, I might add, was parked in a public deck that was offering free parking until construction was completed. Unanimously we agreed that we deserved dessert, so we ducked into one of the local cafés. The busy baristas waited on an amiable line composed of generations X and Y. We got our coffee and treats and went back out to the street, just in time to see fireworks in the distance. In essence, three adults parked, were entertained for a few hours, and had dessert for about ten bucks total. I can see why my sister loves this town.

The only thing left to do was go back to Heidi's apartment to relax. We flopped on the couch and basked in the glow of red Christmas lights. Slowly designers are discovering what young adults have known for years: the best solution to cost-effective mood lighting is the $2.00 strand of Christmas lights. We visited late into the night, and then went to sleep. It was cozy and comfortable, and a much appreciated upgrade from a plain motel room in a rainy Texas town. I slung my arm across Senator and passed out.

The next morning we spent a few hours exploring the same hundred square feet of Springfield known as Heidi's living room. At some point one of us proposed that we begin to do something that required movement from the couch. Eventually we all gave in. Our well-rested trio left to go bumming again.

Our first leg of the excursion took us through a well-manicured Victorian neighborhood. Several quaint bed and breakfasts were mixed in. A few blocks away stood an old Gothic Episcopal church. Stone arches lined the side wing and the windows. It was pretty, but it deserved to be set in a stony field in England. Leaving that neighborhood, we made one more stop at a local park to walk through the gardens. Though positioned next to a junk yard, they were attractive nonetheless.

Our final stop on the tour may surprise readers who know us. Though we love the outdoors and find a cool night in the woods exhilarating, we are hardly the typical Bass Pro Shop patrons. Fishing and hunting rank about #4,962 on our list of hobbies. The giant Bass Pro outlet store in Springfield, however, is a viable sort of entertainment.

It was Saturday afternoon and the parking lot was packed with every SUV and pick up truck known to man. RVs and boats had a healthy representation as well. Heidi pulled her Cavalier in between two vehicles that looked like they could eat it (and us) for lunch. Apparently these were not people suffering from the media-hyped economic crunch.

Once inside the wood and stone castle, you immediately realize that you are not in a store, but some sort of mountain man Disneyland. The 'you are here' map displayed the multi-floor plan that included waterfalls, aquariums, a food court, a Starbucks (in case you could not make it to the food court), a shooting range, a giant stuffed (as in taxidermy, not plush) bear, and a boat showroom. The crowds were thick with locals and tourists of all ages. Come to think of it, the crowds were thick, period. I guess hunting and fishing are not very physical sports; there tends to be a lot of down time.

We opted to go to the aquariums. Meandering along a stone path, past the brook (all indoors), we arrived in a quiet theatre with a wall-sized aquarium. Swimming around inside were rare fish that were native to the Ozark region. As we were admiring their grace, another customer vocalized her impression. "Wow! I just want to EAT that!" she exclaimed. Clearly this was not a vegetarian's playground.

We then walked to the camping section. *Okay, this is a little closer to our territory.* I browsed the sleeping bags that guaranteed to keep you alive in sub-zero temperatures. Who buys these? Chances are, if you plan to go camping and you notice that the forecast predicts a low of -20°F, you will postpone your trip until the mercury climbs to a fiery 30°F or so. Ergo, the bag is unnecessary. On the other hand, if you are not planning to camp, but a horrendous catastrophe befalls you while you are outside, and the temperature drops to a nippy -20°F, chances are you will not happen to have a sleeping bag with you in your spare pocket. Either way, the product is superfluous.

I was actually in search of a storage bag to hold our tent and its accessories. Would you believe I could find nothing appropriate? The lesson is that bigger is not always better. We mosied out of the camping section, toward the gourmet snack section.* Briefly I was tempted by the salsas. How could you resist checking out condiments with such alluring names as Fartless Bean Salsa or Kick-Ass Hot Sauce?

We continued on. Squirming our way through the crowds I heard a man ask his friend if he had seen his wife. "If I could find a NASCAR section, then I know she'd be there..." It was time to leave. Bass Pro Shop was fun, but I felt a little like a fish out of water and mounted on someone's wall. Although, for inexplicable reasons, I have been receiving monthly copies of Field & Stream in the mail. I have never subscribed and I have no idea how they got may name or address. Perhaps they have me confused with Hemingway.

Back at Heidi's we started a mildly competitive Scrabble game. The sky darkened and the wind picked up, raising the drama. My sister had recently earned certification as an official storm spotter. She instantly went into meteorological mode, explaining which clouds where going where and why. We all stepped outside for a better view. Various shades of gray swirled overhead as the wind slapped the vertical blinds around. A violent storm followed, with the sun and blue skies on its heels. When it comes to weather, Springfield supposedly has the distinction of being one of the most unpredictable cities in the United States. I could believe it. I changed between jeans and shorts three times that day.

When things settled down, we ran between the remaining drops and jumped in the car. All day long we had saved our

---

*No, I have no idea why this exists, so don't bother asking.

appetite for Lambert's Cafe, the famous 'Home of Throwed Rolls'. I expounded on Lambert's in the last chapter, and the roll throwin' was still going strong. In fact, one hit me in the head and split in half upon impact. I was only sorry that half fell to the floor. The food is still delicious, and still nonstop. Have as much as you want, and head's up!

Some people go for after-dinner mints. Heidi took us for after-dinner books. *Boy does my sister know me.* Another quirky delight of Springfield is the Library Center. While the library is your average city library, in the foyer they host a gift shop. In addition to various upscale and clever gifts, the shop sells used library books. Once a week titles are pulled and relegated to the store's shelves. Prices are excellent, service is friendly, and the money goes to back into the library. Why doesn't every library do this?

The time with my sister had come and gone too fast yet again. Sunday morning we packed up and said goodbye. As if Missouri wanted to give us a dark souvenir, we witnessed a bad accident on the way home. Of course, it was caused by one of their notorious drivers attempting a dangerous lane change. There were no fatalities, but plenty of debris landed around the road in what looked like a slow motion movie clip. We could not get home fast enough.

The remainder of the drive went by relatively quickly, and before we knew it, we were home. In one massive relay, we unloaded the car completely. To my chagrin, the back seat had not dried from the water incident three days earlier. Oops. It probably would have helped if we took the cooler off of it so it could have dried. I had more bad visions of bills from the rental company. *Let's see, with the chip in the window, and the water damaged back seat...*

There was no time to properly dry it, so I did my best to soak it up with old towels. It was time to return the car, but I reasoned that no one would be there to inspect it for another twelve hours or so. I rolled down all four windows completely, got on the country road, picked up my speed, and hoped for the best. My plan actually worked, because by the time we completed the half hour drive, the seat was completely dry. *Water, what water?* As for the chip in the windshield, the numerous bug guts must have camouflaged it well, because the company called the next day to say thank you and that they appreciated my business.

On the way home we stopped to pick up a pizza. Inside, the local little league team was celebrating their victory with pizza, pop, and the opportunity to riotously drive their coaches nuts. When our pizza was done, we stepped up to the counter to pay. The owner smiled when he recognized us. Yes, we were back in our small plot on the planet. We returned home with just enough of an evening left to fall asleep to a B horror movie. *Hello, Bela. Did you miss us?...*

Chapter 3
Death's Door, and Other Fun Portals: Early July 2008

I once read a statistic that said that more than half of United States residents live within ninety miles of an ocean. Think about that for a moment. Now look at a map. Open your thumb and index finger just about *that* much. Lay them along the coasts. That is half of the population, leaving the rest of us to occupy the great sprawling land between. So my odds were 50/50, and I happened to be born among the landlubbers. Nevertheless, there is an unquenchable part of me that desperately wants to live along the northern shores of the violent and beautiful Atlantic. The culture, literature, history, and attitude of New England all attract me on numerous levels, making it my own private dreamland.

Alas, trips to New England require sufficient time off, planning, and fundage; Illinoisans cannot just hop in a car and drop by Connecticut for the weekend. Happily, at some point in time and space God took pity on us, creating a special place that would serve as a retreat from the prairie. Thus, Door County exists. Its miles of rugged shoreline, quaint farms and towns, and heritage as a shipping community earn it the nickname 'Cape Cod of the Midwest'. We, the people of the Great Lakes states, affectionately embrace it.

I had been to Door County twice before, seeing the popular sites, and driving the circle around the peninsula. Senator, on the other hand, knew almost nothing about the area, so I was anxious to introduce him to it. So it was with great delight that he and I accepted an invitation from our friends to join them at a farmhouse in Door County for a few days. We would meet Bill and Marge for a few days of biking, booking, and basking along beaches. Just a few weeks after returning from our trip to the southwest, we loaded up Trucky and headed toward northeastern Wisconsin.

The morning that we left was cloudy, rainy, and drearily lacking in that vacation feel. The forecast was not promising either, for two kids excited to play outside as much as possible over the next few days. In spite of the weather, we were looking forward to visiting our friends, and we wanted to get past the drive. Why is it that the road *to* somewhere always feels longer than the trip home? We continued to drive north past a hell of a lot of corn, and finally saw something interesting to break up the monotony.

Stopped along the opposite side of traffic was an extremely long trailer. On that trailer was one blade from a windmill propeller. In the past five to ten years, harnessing wind power has become popular around the Midwest and Plains regions. This, for many reasons, is a good thing. Aesthetically, though, one wonders. Far from the picturesque symbols of olden day family farms, these windmills are giant, white, multi-armed towers, arranged in gangs. There is no romance in these machines, only raw, sleek power and function. Seeing one lying horizontal on the ground only reinforced this idea.*

I wish I could report that there were other amazing sites along the route, but soon enough we entered the southern tip of the county. Door County is large, as far as counties go. It is an elongated peninsula that stretches a good fifty miles from tip to tip. To the west is Green Bay and to the east is Lake Michigan. At the north end of the county, the waters meet. At the south end of the county, Packer fans put their personal prejudices aside, allowing Illinois visitors to access this playground and leave their tourism dollars behind.

Once you cross into the county, the towns immediately take on a nautical theme. Boat slips and marinas dot the shore at regular intervals. Seafood is a staple. Though I have my doubts that whales regularly lost their way and somehow followed the St. Lawrence Seaway inland through the maze of Great Lakes and ended up in Wisconsin, the sense of rooted sea ports is definitely there. (You can call me Ishmael.)

Our destination was about 2/3 of the way 'up' the peninsula, so we decided on the Lake Michigan side, and meandered our way through a handful of towns before finding our turnoff. The biggest distinction we noticed was the variable temperature. There was a brisk breeze off the lake shore, dropping the temperature at least 10°F. Moving inland, even just a few blocks in some cases, it was considerably warmer. Leaving the windows down, you could feel the changes as though you were swimming through different currents. I enjoyed the unpredictability.

---

*About ten miles south of our town, there is a group of these mills, and from the bluffs it looks like we are being invaded. They are particularly dramatic on a winter night, when the bare trees leave the view fully exposed, with the windmills' red lights blinking out a warning to low-flying planes and People of Earth in general.

When we came to County Road F, we turned, trading the crowds for the quiet rustic setting of the interior county. In some states, including Wisconsin, the county roads are called by letter. What happens, you may wonder, when a county has more than the prescribed twenty-six letters of the English alphabet? Simple-- they double the letters with names like EE or NN. To a five-year old's endless satisfaction, I believe there is even a County PP.

From here the directions took on that sketchy charm so common to rural areas. *Go a little ways, and follow the bend around a farm. Well, you know, not a great big farm, but a sizable one. Travel up the road a piece, past Mrs. Bjornsson's lovely perennial garden. (Have you seen her roses this year? I mean, they're nothing like Mrs. Toleffson's were in '96, but still gorgeous, you know.) Anyway, keep going until you're about halfway across th'other side, and then you'll pass the weaver's shop. After this, look for us on the left. There's no address as far as you know.*

We believed we were closing in on our destination. Senator slowed down to a pioneering tourist pace, and we craned our necks to scrutinize the scenery for clues. As our investigation was underway, a man sailed by on a bicycle. We looked at each other. "Was that Bill that just went by?" Senator asked.

I thought it was, but I was not sure. "There's only one way to find out," I responded. Either we would easily be led right to the farmhouse, or some poor soul on a bike would be unintentionally stalked by us. Thankfully, it was Bill.

He led us to the driveway of a spacious white farmhouse. Once parked, we immediately noticed more mature versions of many of the plants that we had introduced to our gardens at home, earlier in the year. In the side yard, seated at a picnic table were Marge and her mother, Del. Birds darted from feeder to feeder, trading stories of where to get the best seed. I vaguely remember a swing swaying in the breeze, unconcerned with our arrival. The scene was inviting, and so comfortable that it felt as though we were being welcomed by friends who had been patiently expecting us for years.

Our first order of business was a proper introduction to Del. As stated, she is our friend Marge's mother, and one of the reasons that so many of our friends are decades older than us. While you might mistake her for 'just another nice older lady at the grocery store', to do so would be to cheat yourself. Del's stories, as well as her thoughtful perspectives and conversation entertained us for a great portion of our stay. Whether it's discussing classic film or our hometown's historical mob connections, Del is a vivid source of knowledge and creativity secretly packed into a quiet, petite, gentle package. This was going to be a fun trip.

Bill led us inside the house. Much of Door County lodging centers around the bed & breakfast culture. While b&bs are romantic, elegant, and stately, they can also be a bit austere. If the object of your trip to Door County is to sip champagne while snuggling on an authentic Nineteenth Century courting sofa near the fire, or to soak in a whirlpool filled with rose petals, then you should definitely choose a bed & breakfast. As none of these were our reasons for visiting the Door, however, the farmhouse was the perfect type of lodging.

The home, which Bill and Marge have rented every summer for years, was decorated in early-1970s style, with that return to rusticity that brought woodwork back to the forefront, if a little awkwardly. Plenty of bedrooms held plenty of beds. The great room offered seating for at least a dozen, in addition to the large dining room table that could accommodate a family, their friends, and probably even a few enemies. In short, there was no fussiness. No signs hinted at check-out times or reminded us to be quiet for the sake of other roomers. One could drop a dirty dish in the sink without feeling like he had defiled the atmosphere. If a lost little bug happened to wander in, you either stepped on it or tossed it outside, and then went on with your life. Come to think of it, I don't even recall seeing a coaster.

We chose a bedroom and made up a bed, complete with our favorite blankie from home. Moments later we joined the others to peruse a few travel guides and decide on the afternoon's agenda. Herein lies one of the curious facts about your author. I am always anxious to flip through travel brochures. Somehow I believe that they hold a mysterious cache of secrets that will be revealed to me, a stranger in a strange land, thereby enhancing my vacation experience. In reality, I find that they uselessly hold only the following: 1.)advertisements for ludicrously overpriced hotels, 2.)advertisements for disturbingly underpriced motels, usually containing some combination of the words 'bayside' or 'harbor' or 'view' or 'top' or 'sand', 3.)information on wind surfing, regardless of geographical region, 4.)a list of the best steakhouses, 5.)a full page color ad for the best outboard motor repair shop in the state, 6.)personal ads (suggesting that these poor souls have exhausted every option in their town, and now must lure in tourists), and 7.)the Calendar of Events from three summers ago. I have yet to learn my lesson and save myself time. Alas, the pictures are pretty, and I am sucked in.

Despite the brochures, we all settled on wandering through some shops. Piling into the car, we drove a few miles to the west side of the peninsula, bordered by Green Bay. By now, Reader, you must know that I generally detest shopping. Browsing gift shops with many overly cute and superfluous items with four other inventive characters becomes an experience in its own right, though.

We entered the standard candle store, which sported at least twenty versions of Christmas scents, as well as a few Hanukkah aromas. Just when we thought we had inhaled all that the month of December could offer, we turned the corner and beheld the Christmas store. For some reason, Christmas stores are a tourism fundamental in the upper Midwest. Perhaps they try to make the most of their central location between the North Pole and the Equator. Whatever the reason, they boast all things Yuletide, from delicate glass ornaments, to pillows stitched with ugly reindeer that are manufactured for the sole purpose of giving to grade school teachers. As a high school teacher, I am excluded from such gifts, but I'm sure Marge would agree with my theory.*

The last shop in the strip was devoted strictly to imports from England. Are you in need of a new pair of (London) tube socks? Getting a bit low on dinnerware with the queen's face imprinted upon it? How about a Buckingham Palace replica as a conversation piece? This is your place. While it is true I am an earnest Anglophile, I could not find anything worth buying here. I tried, hard, but none of the pub logos grabbed me, and I could just as easily purchase a *Fawlty Towers* dvd online. Something in my heart just would not allow me to buy British souvenirs in Wisconsin. Or maybe that was Senator. "Let's wait until we actually go to England." It sounded like great advice to me, although the last time we tried that, we ended up in the Dakotas (see *How to Read a Compass in the Dark*).

The shopping adventure ended with nary a purchase among us. Now the idea of eating was gradually sown in our midst. Given the casual nature of our group, meals were decided when one of us felt hungry, someone else hemmed and hawed that he agreed, a third person went so far as to make a suggestion of what/where to eat, and the rest of us did not have any strong opinion otherwise. At some point Bill mentioned going to Al Johnson's for an early dinner.

---

*Marge is, plainly put, the World's Greatest Kindergarten Teacher. She will humbly reject this title if she reads this, but it's true. She is upbeat, fun, intelligent, patient, realistic, cool-headed, and, as of this printing, she has never once used duct tape to quell a wailing child, nor left a kid behind on a field trip-- even accidentally! She is truly amazing.

65

The Door County crowd knows Al Johnson's as the restaurant with the goats on the roof. In Chicago, this might be seen as a problem, but there it is a novelty. The restaurant's Swedish theme includes a grass-covered roof, perfect for grazing goats. Within the building, the grazing is just as good for humans. Ever in search of new and satisfying cheeses, Senator and I ordered grilled cheese sandwiches. Forget the side dishes-- this was a two-hander classic that dripped and stretched from the plate to the palate.

After dinner we drove back to the house to lay around and digest. I started to read a book that I had brought, but was instead absorbed into a game of dominoes with Del. Tiles and dots-- who would think it could get so competitive? The early evening slipped into later evening, and Marge suggested we go watch the sun set over the bay.

Apparently we were not the only ones with this idea, because the shoreline was filled with families and couples staring out westward at the great widescreen of nature. Bill pointed out a Chinese junque ship on the horizon. In my ignorance I pictured a floating flea market. As it turns out, a 'junque' is a beautiful sailboat, wrongly translated from a Chinese symbol meaning lake or river, due to its pronunciation *'jung'*.* Leave it to modern English.

When the sun had set, the stars took prominence. We returned to the farmhouse and Bill made fire in the back yard while Marge gathered drinks in the kitchen. Five of us adjusted our tree stumps and encircled a blazing fire that seemed to keep changing direction, despite the lack of wind. Conversation ranged from small talk to the planning of a radio show we would collectively write, enact, and produce, in the spirit of the 1940s. Though we have yet to achieve this, I could see it feasibly happening in the near future. I fantasized myself in a street-

---

*See www.scalemodel.net/Gallery/Chineseship.aspx

length dress, hair neatly pinned beneath a stylish hat, falling into curls at my shoulders. I hoped I would get to play a two-faced vamp. Short girls never get to play vamps, even on the radio...

When the last of the embers blinked out, we went inside for the final treat of the evening. In 2007 Bill and Marge founded the 16mm Movie Club. Requirements for membership include wearing a club pin, partaking of junk (or junque) food, and a healthy appreciation of World War II-era action serials. As a vacation special, Bill showed *The Perils of Nyoka*. Nyoka, the heroine, experienced the inconvenient perils associated with outwitting various Arabian thieves and murderers while fashionably dressed in a sort of sexed-up boy scout outfit. While we did not complete all fifteen episodes, I saw enough to learn never to trust anyone who is not American. With visions of girl-next-door heroism dancing in our heads, we retired for the evening.

Wednesday was designated as Washington Island day. If you go to the north end of Door County and forget to stop, you will end up in either Green Bay or Lake Michigan, depending which side of the line you sink beneath. If, however, you consult a ferry schedule, you can take the thirty minute trip across the water known as 'Death's Door'[*] and disembark at Washington Island. As one might imagine, there is not much on Washington Island, and there are not many cars to get in a cyclist's way. Taking advantage of these facts, we checked our bikes on the ferry and climbed to the upper deck.

When we docked, Del split from us to take a tram tour and Marge became our guide, leading us first to a rocky beach. The air was still cool, but it was warm in the sunshine. We walked out toward the water and watched the clear waves slap against the rocks. Here, a fruit break was in order. As we sat

---

[*]In its maritime past, this spot was notorious for sinking ships, earning it the moniker 'Death's Door', from which the county takes its name.

down on the picnic table, though, we were attacked by a persistent pair of flies. When they got the best of us, we left the beach.

To get back to the main road, we had to pump our way up a small hill. When doing this on a bike, the rider has to concentrate, looking down toward the ground rather than out toward the path. This set us up well for our science fiction moment. Around the curve, descending the hill toward us, came a roving gang of Segway riders.

Helmet-donned and posture-perfect, these terrors zipped right by us, ignoring our desperate laugh-induced gasps for air. This was too hilarious for words. Thank God there's finally a solution for people who desire short-distance forward propulsion without having to exert effort. If you ever imagined an invasion from a planet of yuppie tourists, I'm sure it looked exactly like this. The sad part is that they would be able to easily overtake us as we were immobilized by the laughter.

Recovery was not easy, but we made it. With sore abdomens, we rode to the lookout tower. Marge preferred to stay on solid ground, but Senator, Bill, and I climbed several stories on the rickety wooden stairs. At the top, the vista was breathless-- we assume.

It wasn't easy to see past the obnoxious couple who managed to simultaneously block 270° of the 360° of panorama while talking on their cell phones. *Please, God, just let her drop it.* I stared at her hand, watching for any sign of a slip up, but no such luck. Too bad; it would have been beautiful. Eventually they moved out of the way of Wisconsin. Now I realize, Reader, that there are stupid people everywhere, and I accept this.[*] What I cannot understand, though, is what would possess such folks to climb high into the air to profess their self-centeredness. Maybe

---

[*] I do wish, however, that they would stop reproducing, but that is another matter altogether.

they were looking for enlightenment. Maybe they were looking for their car. Maybe they just had really crappy cell phone reception. *Can you hear me now?* Of course, I got over it, but it still would have been satisfying to see that phone plunge down into the trees. Does that make me a bad person?...

The next stop was the haunted nightclub. Although, technically we did not have proof that the abandoned building was haunted, or even a night club for that matter, Bill proposed the theory, Marge seconded it, and it was unanimously decided. The two-story stone and wood structure sat at a lonely crossroads, surrounded by fields and prairie. It was three or four times the size of an average family home, providing plenty of room for dancing and such, we postulated. The windows were ancient. Some held cracks, others spiders. Either suited our sequence nicely. The second story even had a door that opened out to a verandah. This, of course, would allow the spirits to step out under the stars when they needed a break from dancing. It would also serve as a means of disposing of out-of-control hoodlums if necessary. Here, again, I refer to my previous comments regarding travel brochures. You would never find this place in one of them. *When, oh when, will I learn?*

After a brief ice cream stop, we met Del at the ferry and loaded up for the return ride. When we took our seats on the top deck, another pesky fly found us. Actually, he was more brutal than pesky, chomping at any exposed skin he could find. This prompted Bill to sing a song he once wrote while being bitten by just such a fly. I won't spoil his genius by giving away his lyrics here, but suffice it to say, references to the queen, a nudist, and Soleil Moon Frye can all be found in the tune *Bitey the Fly*.

On the way back to the house, we stopped in a small book store. There are fewer and fewer independent booksellers these days. I don't imagine too many people can make a living at this. Still, in small pockets of the country, they hold their position as curious houses of knowledge, entertainment, and marvelously musty book dust.

It was now time again for the ritual vacation nap. Everyone quietly dispersed to a bed or a soft chair. Senator dozed as I read. Then I dozed as he read. The only noises came from a few ambitious birds trying to balance on a feeder outside.

At some point someone brought up Mexican food. Now we were awake. Our friends took us to a place they enjoyed, and we ordered something hot and cheesy. The curious thing about Mexican food is that you cannot judge it by its proximity to Mexico. For example, we had the worst Mexican food of our lives in Texas. It's true. Now in Wisconsin, at the opposite end of the country, we had what may have been our favorite Mexican meal of all time. There's a moral in here somewhere. If you can't find it, just be sure to go heavy on the jalapeño and cumin.

When the sun went down it was time for round two under the stars. We chatted again about everything and nothing, and part of the pleasure was that most of it was forgettable. It was true relaxation. It was funny how we were not that far from either populated coast of the county, but here in the middle it was so dark and quiet. The location was a well-kept secret.

It had been a long day and I was tired, but like the others, I was soon glued to the television when Bill loaded the dvd player. Nyoka's latest perils kept me up another hour or so. We then climbed the steep stairs to our bedroom and collapsed on the bed. The weather forecast had predicted rain for all three days. So far we had cheated it. Hopefully we could squeeze in one more day of biking.

Thursday morning the sun woke us up through our east window. That was a promising sign. We then noticed the smell of freshly brewed coffee wafting up the stairs. Good morning, indeed! In keeping with the kick-back spirit of the house, we dressed and joined our hosts for a makeshift buffet à la kitchen counter. I wanted to contribute some sort of snack or food item, but I was not sure what to bring. Then, the day before we left, I invented my fallback for all future vacations involving the hospitality of others. I baked spice muffins, packed finger-sized pieces of fresh fruit, and sliced up a variety of cheeses. After all, who doesn't love guests that come bearing gifts of cheese? (If you can also convince Bill to come along with you and make his delectable waffles, you are sure to be a hit!)

After breakfast we loaded up the bikes and drove a few miles to Peninsula State Park. I had camped there years ago, and I remembered hiking the rugged cliffs that overlooked Green Bay. I also vaguely remembered a lighthouse on one of the park's shores. What I did not remember were the ridiculous daily fees Wisconsin charges to use their state parks.

Here, the ever-capable Marge taught me a sneaky trick. If you park outside the entrance to the park and ride your bicycle in on the path, no one will stop you for permits or fees. *Way to stick it to the Man!* So we did just that, leaving the cars on the main street.

The four of us zipped away, dodging small children and large adults, neither of whom seemed comfortable on two wheels. Within a half hour on this paved trail, one encounters sunny meadow, dense forest, a backdrop of cliffs, turns, small hills, a few road crossings, and just for good measure, a speed bump or two. Without missing a beat, we sped single file through the terrain. I'd like to see the Segway gang pull that off!

Our first stop was the lighthouse. I am sure it had an official name, but that was not the focus of the stop. We parked our bikes, reapplied sunscreen, and stretched our legs. Near the short path to the lighthouse was a giant anchor. Tugging at the end of the giant anchor was a straining, gritting Bill, posing for the camera.

Of course, we thought the shot of a man of super-human strength pulling an enormous anchor out of the ground was hysterical. The dozens of tourists milling about weren't so sure.

To look at some of their faces you would think they had never seen four fully-grown adults uncontrollably amused at their own fully-grown imaginations. They had a lot to learn. I felt sorry for them-- and even sorrier for their children.

We hopped on our bikes and continued to the beach. The breeze made the air a little too chilly to wade, but the rain was holding off. We nibbled some snacks and visited a while before speeding off again. Just as easily as we had entered, we slipped out of the park and rode to our cars.

Getting into our car, I assumed we would follow Bill and Marge back to the house. Senator hesitated. I followed his gaze, and I knew what he was thinking. "No, no, no. I don't want you getting any ideas," I protested. What are the odds that we had parked fifty feet from a bike shop that just happened to sell skis, after he had been threatening to buy me a pair for the past two years?

"Shut up," he stated simply. The only time he ever uses that phrase with me is when he is going to buy something for me or us. He went in to 'check things out' while I waited in the car. It wasn't that I did not want them; we had gone cross-country skiing once and I loved it. It's just that I am very uncomfortable with someone else making a major purchase for me. Analyze that all you want, Reader, but it's not likely to change anytime soon.

As I was carefully formulating my rebuttal, Senator's head popped out of the front door of the shop. He did not say a word, opting instead for the authoritative head nod and flick of the pointer finger, indicating that I should join him in the store. As it turned out, we found a good deal on skis, poles, and boots in my size. One satisfied Senator, one grateful sales clerk, and one perplexed Wendy V later, we emerged. My boy arranged the equipment in the back of our truck bed, giving two states the impression that we had attempted to go for a snow holiday in the middle of July.

Back at the house we met Bill, Marge, and Del again. Senator relayed our find, and they promptly took his side. I was a beaten woman, and admitted defeat accordingly. After some time to read and sprawl, we ventured out to another lighthouse at Cana Island.

The Cana Island lighthouse is positioned so that, depending on rainfall and tide time, you may have to wade out to it. On that day, the rocky trail leading to it was above water, making the lighthouse easily accessible. Feeling adventurous, Bill and I decided we would take the winding staircase to the top of the house. There was a small charge, so we approached the ticket booth to purchase a pass. The booth was tiny, making traffic toll booths seem like luxury suites.

Inside was an elderly man who took his vocation as ticket taker seriously. He explained the rules, took our cash, and then, with regret, he noticed my shoes. "Oh, Miss," he intoned gravely, "You can't go up there with open-toed shoes." I had not really considered my velcro hiking sandals to be open-toed, but there was no swaying this gentleman. He was hired to protect wayward and haphazard souls like myself from tripping and spiraling down the metal steps to demise due to foolish choice of footwear. Initially annoyed, I soon realized that this must be my guardian angel. He gave me back my money, encouraging me to come back another day when I was wearing tennis shoes.

As Bill and his correctly shod toes ascended inside the lighthouse, the rest of us walked out to the rock beach beneath. The waves crashed against the shore and we found suitable sitting rocks. A few sandpipers played tag with the tide. The rain had held off for our outdoor activities, but the Door County sky was gradually turning that wonderful gray-blue-green of distant New England coasts.

Eventually Bill came out at the top, waving to us from behind the railing. Unfortunately, even his shoes could not save him from scraping the top of his head at one of the turns in the lighthouse. Though now a millimeter or two shorter, he was more determined than ever to set up a few perfect shots. Positioning his camera on the railing, he took our picture down below. Thankfully, his return trip was less painful.

For our last Door dinner, we tried a local tavern. As in the case of most taverns, the food was honest, straightforward, local, and fried. By that I mean deep fried, and served in plastic baskets with paper that never has the remotest chance of being able to soak up the entire grease puddle. So do not be misled when I say that we had a platter of vegetables for dinner. Believe it or not, places like this make it possible to be a chunky vegetarian. We feasted on zucchini, cauliflower, potatoes, mushrooms, onions, and many other items that journeyed straight from the garden to the fat fryer. It was divine.

When our feast concluded, we agreed that a short walk was in order. Like any major tourist region, Door County's main roads are lined with all of life's nonessentials, from antiques to boutiques. The incredible part occurred while waiting outside one of the shops for our friends. We were talking with Del when I looked up and saw, of all people, my high school geometry teacher. I won't admit how long I have been out of high school, but it has been long enough that I found it miraculous that she had not changed, and that she remembered me. In fact, she asked if I had gone to the college I had planned to attend, and what I was doing now. I practically tripped over my words telling her that I now taught high school, too. Coincidences like that hold a lot of meaning for me. I guess I should not have been surprised, though, having also just met my guardian angel that same afternoon.

The evening was too damp for a fire, but there was plenty of time for one final session of dominoes. Five competitive kids from three generations drew dots, played dots, saw dots, and cursed dots in turn. After the game, it seemed that Nyoka had once again found herself in peril. We watched her take on more

Hollywood Arabians before retiring for the night. Us, that is, not her. I'm sure she never sleeps.

    Friday morning was drizzly and overcast. We could not complain, though. It had only rained on the days we had to drive. We shared breakfast and coffee with our friends again. I had particularly enjoyed getting to know Del. We would see all three of them a few more times over the summer at the 16mm Movie Club.* For now though, it was time to pack our snow skis and other summer gear and head home.

    The drive was boring, but the conversation of two friends sharing a carriage home was enjoyable. Thankful for a great trip, we entered our home and unpacked. Realizing we were both hungry, we brainstormed a few options for dinner. Our decision was soon made for us. Less than an hour after we had arrived home, the power went out. *What was that we had been saying about not having any catastrophes or inconveniences surrounding our trips?* It seemed that our vacations were back to their old mischief again. Hopefully, we could squeeze one more trip in before I had to go back to being a real adult with a real job.

---

*No Nazis allowed!

Chapter 4
Welcome Back:
Early August 2008

We had traveled in June and July, so I figured we might as well do my first summer as a teacher right, and travel in August as well. Though I started back August 2nd, there was one four-day weekend squeezed between registration and the first day of school. The price of airline tickets had more than doubled from the previous trip, but we were anxious to get back to New York so we booked a flight. Though this would be our sixth New York excursion, we would be staying in Brooklyn this time, instead of Manhattan.

I must admit, I had mixed feelings about the unfamiliar borough. We had become very comfortable with Lower Manhattan and Midtown. Long ago had we ditched the street maps and subway guides. Though it somewhat unnerved my boyfriend, I could even trek down to the juice bar or swing by Trinity Church on my own, rejoining him in time for a casual coffee. It was fun to walk by the ivy-covered brick row houses of Greenwich Village and have tourists stop and ask for directions. *No, actually you are nowhere near Battery Park.*

Now we would be the new kids again, concentrating on street signs and landmarks as we tried to memorize the layout of neighborhoods. Our friends Spencer and Michelle had taken the plunge and moved across the river, gaining more space. The last time we had seen their place, it was under construction. There were no interior walls, and debris from the renovation lay around in piles. Despite our love of Manhattan, we were excited for them, and we could not wait to see the transformed renovation of their new home.

There was another first for this trip to New York. We had always found the best air fare deals from Midway to La Guardia via ATA. This time, however, we would fly Delta. Why? That would be because a few months earlier, literally overnight, ATA declared bankruptcy and halted all flights. They gave no notice, and many passengers were left stranded.* Thus went the economy in 2008.

On a warm, pleasant morning, exactly one month after leaving for Door County, we went through the routine, found our new airline, and boarded the plane. Though we were on a small aircraft, it was half empty (or half full, if you are an economic optimist). Senator nuzzled into one side of me and promptly fell asleep. How I envy people who can sleep so easily on flights... I instead, settled in with my current book group selection.

The day was clear and bright, but you would never have known it from our takeoff. We roared upward, bouncing our way through thousands of feet. Twenty minutes into the flight we were still jerking and bumping through an agitated state of turbulence or pilot inexperience. I silently hoped it was not the latter. It had been sixteen months since we last flew anywhere, the greatest gap since we began traveling together. Maybe I was just a little nervous, or perhaps I had forgotten how it felt. My thoughts were interrupted with another roller coaster drop.

---

*I assume, however, that the planes in flight finished their routes. I don't recall any tales of kicking people overboard at 30,000 feet.

Nope, this was a rocky flight. Enough already! It did eventually smooth out somewhat, but there was no love lost between the passengers and the wild blue yonder by the time we landed.

In the baggage terminal we watched for our faithful single piece of luggage. Among those waiting to intercept their (or someone else's) bags were several obnoxious convention types. You know the kind. Thirty-eightish, pushy. Ecstatic to be free from the boss for a few days while still getting paid. Ecstatic to be free from the wife for a few days while still getting laid. Feels the need to speak loudly and name-drop to overcompensate for any range of inferiorities including, but not limited to, those in the genitalia region. Senator rolled his eyes, and I thanked God that I had the brains not to go for a Convention Boy. We were glad to see our bag finally emerge from the rubber curtain and come gliding our way. In an instant he scooped it up and we went outside to meet Michelle.

It was great to be back. I glued my eyes to the window as we drove through new territory. Blocks of graffiti welcomed us to the land of my teaching inspiration, Gabe Kotter. I briefly thought of the new batch of 'sweat hogs' I would inherit for the next nine months. What would they be like? Would the year run smoothly? Would they get along with each other? I quickly admonished myself not to care for the next four days, and joined the conversation already in progress in the front seat. The three of us continued to brainstorm reasons why 95% of modern rock stinks, at last arriving in Williamsburg.

Spencer and Michelle now occupy the penthouse dwelling of a seven-story building. The two-bedroom home is surrounded by windows overlooking Brooklyn and the east coast of Manhattan. The bright red trim and its position next to a large, railed sun deck give the impression that the home is a boat house floating high above the river. While a tree or two *does* grow in Brooklyn, none approach seven stories. Still, being inside the home feels a little like hiding out in a tree house, especially when the wind whips through the windows.

We settled in briefly and then walked back down to the street with Michelle and her dogs. That particular day (8/8/08), a rare musical event was taking place. Eighty-eight drummers would perform an eighty-eight minute piece in a drum circle (or spiral, as the case was) simultaneously in New York and Los Angeles. I'm not sure why the composer, Yamantaka Eye, had such a fascination with the number eight, but it seemed to work. We walked the few blocks to the waterfront just in time to watch them rehearse.

Drummers are funny creatures. They are an intense breed, given to rhythmic outbursts and, if not properly contained, flailings that would rival a Southern Baptist gospel choir on a hot summer Sunday morning. They are sullen, recognizing their neglected seated position at the rear of the band, but they are not bitter, generally speaking. Rather, they take pride in the fact that 1.)their beat provides the foundation of the song, and 2.)no other musician will ever come close to matching their incredible biceps.

Watching eighty-eight volunteer drummers of various shapes, size, genders, and levels of talent is an afternoon's entertainment in itself. Some drummers were quite good, inhabiting the music freely and comfortably. Others were competent, but one could appreciate their devotion and love of the instrument and the piece. Finally, as expected, some were simply... humans who happened to own a set of drums. Please note, the fliers advertised eighty drummers, not necessarily eighty-eight people who could drum. Overall though, it was an enjoyable spectacle to watch, and it was interesting to listen to the music as the conductor filled one section of the spiral with sound, then let it fade while another area swelled.

When we had had our fill of the rhythmic pounding, we walked another fifteen minutes or so to a sandwich shop. Since delis abound in New York City, a lunch counter has to make its distinction somehow. This particular spot did so by offering a full vegetarian and vegan lunch menu. If you ever have the urge to try an orangish tofu faux egg salad sandwich, hop the next subway to Brooklyn. It was delicious, but thank goodness we were not in any hurry. Even though there were only a few people in the place, it took forever to get our order. I began to think they had to chase down the tofu and kill it to make our sandwich. Nevertheless, yummy.

By this time we were long overdue for a vacation nap. Together we made up a bed in the extra room and slid the corner windows open, letting the wind swirl through. I scrunched a t-shirt over my eyes to block out the sun, and in minutes we were both out. A solid two hours later we awoke. I took a moment to recollect my understanding of where I was. *Hhmmm. Senator's next to me. That's good. This is not our home. We are several stories above street level. I smell the garlic of local restaurants preparing for the dinner crowd. Of course, New York!*

By this time Spencer had come home from work. We plodded into the living room and greeted him, and listened to Michelle explain the proposed plans for the evening. Since moving to a home with a deck, Spencer had sustained a healthy grilling addiction. He offered to make dinner, but a grocery store trip was in order first.

One of the wonderful things about being on vacation is that even common tasks are fun adventures because they take place in new surroundings, a part of someone else's routine. All four of us piled into Spencer and Michelle's car to head to Fairway in Red Hook, quite possibly the greatest grocery store in the western hemisphere. I have probably mentioned this before, but New York has gorgeous produce. This is a real slap in the face to those of us who live in the Midwest, surrounded by farms. Fairway's selection was ripe, aromatic, and seemingly endless.

In fact, there were more than a few opportunities to compliment the quality of the melons, much to the chagrin of one crabby customer. "Do the melon jokes ever *stop* with you?!" she demanded of Spencer & Company. Shaking her head, she walked away. It wasn't as though we invited her to partake of our PG-13 humor.

The rest of Fairway is composed of mini-markets for meats, delicacies, and all stuff like that there. The crowning glory of this grocery, however, is its view. I kid you not. If you step out the back door of my grocery store of choice at home, you will most likely see a few dumpsters, some broken glass, and perhaps a delivery truck. Exiting the back of Fairway, on the other hand, takes you to a deck that overlooks the water and, in the distance, the Statue of Liberty. God bless America-- Land of the Peas and Home of the Grapes!

Upon returning to their home, we went out on the deck to enjoy the sunset while Spencer proved his skills as Grillmaster. It was kind of chilly for an August night, and the wind dropped the temperature down a few degrees further. Hot savory vegetables were the perfect treat. Most intriguing to me was the grilled raddichio. I had never considered this slightly bitter friend of my salad as a grilled side, but I was hooked. My only disappointment is that I have not been able to duplicate its taste at home. I suppose I will have to wait until next summer to experiment.

It was now time for the featured event of the evening. Somehow or another Michelle had acquired tickets to go see Iggy Pop & The Stooges at a venue called Terminal 5. Watching an overenergized sixty-one-year old rocker sounded like a suitable way to spend an evening, so we piled into the car again. Spencer drove us over the river and through the borough to a parking deck near the club.

The line to get in wrapped around the block. The crowd was definitely in the 30+ category, I'm assuming, due to the scheduled act. Waiting in line, I unzipped my purse to fish out my i.d..[*] When out and about, my trademark is my little velvet 'vacation' purse. It is my hands-free solution because it has a long strap that I can place over my head and angle across my body, and it goes with 99.4% of my wardrobe. It's just big enough to fit the essentials (driver's license, credit card, enough cash for cab fare/small excursion/modest bribe, and a generic pay-as-you-go-but-you-can't-run-out-of-minutes-because-you'll-never-get-decent-reception-if-you-actually-need-it cell phone). Being the devoted girlfriend that I am, I also pack a few herbal supplements that aid with digestion, as Senator sometimes pops a few for his stomach if we are eating out.

It was these small, white, powder-filled capsules in an unmarked baggie that got me stopped in the security line as my purse was searched. *Crap, totally forgot about those.* The very large woman in charge of inspecting the Girl Line demanded an explanation. I thought fast, but the only thing that came was the truth. "They're acidophilus," I snapped, as if it were unthinkable that anyone would go to a concert without them.

Whether she figured I wasn't worth hassling, or she was intrigued by the concept of a club drug that sounded like a Greek temple, she let me pass with a simple comment. "You're not apposa' have dese-- go on." With that Senator glanced back to see what the holdup was. I smiled and joined him and our friends in the extremely crowded lobby.

We surveyed the situation. Admission was a general, standing room only situation, and it was generally body-to-body. When you are short, however, it is more accurately described as body odor-to-body odor. Armpit level is a bad place to be in a sweaty room. We collectively decided, without words, to make our way toward the upper level.

---

[*] If you are someone who has carded me in the last five years, God bless you!

Spying an open area, we started to walk toward it. I didn't notice that Spencer had separated from us. Approaching the vacant spot, a security guard stopped us, explaining that it was V.I.P. seating only. You could have fooled me; it didn't look like anything special, but we started to turn away. Just then we looked over and saw Spencer. "It's okay," he explained to the guard, "They're with me." The gatekeeper apologized and admitted us at once. We passed confidently. This was a classic Spencer move. He had sneaked around the back end and met us at the front, as though he had been waiting to entertain his guests in the reserved area. V.I.P. indeed.

The funny thing about special seating is that, though the view is great, you have to question why some of the people are there. For instance, there was a stuffy late-40s couple in front of us that looked like they were attending the concert as the result of a lost bet. If you can't get excited at a classic punk concert, you should probably check your pulse. For crying out loud, Iggy Pop was shirtless and bouncing all over the stage at sixty-one! Proof yet again that age is a state of mind; if you don't mind, you don't age.*

The show delivered as expected. We had a great time, but I had to feel a little sorry for security as they tried in vain to control a crowd that Iggy encouraged to rush the stage. "Cross the barrier! Cross the barrier!" he challenged. Among those accepting his invitation was the quintessential Iggy Pop wannabe. This scuzzy looking dude also sported only jeans, but with a far more prominent gut hanging over. His hair was just a little too stringy, and his tattoos were just a little too worn, and his rock was just a little too rolled. Still, by the end of the song he was convinced that Iggy was proud to be his soul mate. Eventually Iggy was extracted from the man's embrace. I could

---

*Or, as Groucho Marx once said, "You're only as old as the woman you feel."

only imagine the stories this guy told his friends (cats?) that night.

After the show we made our way out to the street. Ears ringing, we walked to the parking deck, talking over each other and laughing at our V.I.P. status. Spencer retrieved the car and drove us all back to Brooklyn. The only fitting end to a night like that is to open the windows, sprawl out on the bed, and gaze at the Manhattan skyline until sleep takes you under... which doesn't take long.

Saturday morning we were up earlier than expected. Morning sun screaming in is the price you pay for a romantic open view of the night sky. Again, though, it was beautiful. We put ourselves together and joined our friends for Juice.

For fruit/vegophiles, there is juice, and then there is Juice. The former is a bottled concoction cooked and pasteurized beyond all danger or flavor. The latter is a fresh, vital experience. As Michelle's latest toy, the Juicer was employed in full force that morning. Everything went in-- beets, peaches, carrots, greens, and, of course, the great melons. We relaxed on the deck and planned our day. Michelle had errands to run, so Spencer, Senator, and I would walk a dog or two, hit the farmer's market, and reconvene for lunch. We downed the remainder of the nectar and parted ways.

We walked through the neighborhood to the outdoor market at the park. The area, like so many others, is in transition. Everywhere you look buildings are being rehabbed, bought, or sold. The battle against broken glass and graffiti wages on, but the people are real and the streets have their own distinct character. In fact, as a new experiment, one main street was closed on summer weekend afternoons, creating an open mall walkway.

On this particular afternoon, ping pong tables were set up in the middle of the street for a tournament that would take place later. We strolled through and found something for each of us.

Spencer couldn't resist playing an impromptu game with one of the locals. Senator found a chair under a shady tree and you can guess what that led to. Zzzzzz.

I, believe it or not, shopped! Well, technically speaking, I shopped. I was watching Spencer play when I spied a girl about my size selling clothes on the side of the street. Apparently people can obtain permits to set up a street sale like you would hold a garage sale in the suburbs. I walked over to get a better look. Upon closer review I decided that she was almost exactly my size, and she had good taste. In five minutes I purchased seven or eight items from her, totaling a whopping $11. Now if that was all shopping ever entailed, perhaps I would consider it a viable pastime.

Eventually we dragged Spencer away from his ping pong domination and joined Michelle back at the house. The Williamsburg area of Brooklyn has a large Polish population, so it was determined that we should try a Polish cafeteria. I was leery of what I suspected to be meat grease on my potato pierogi (hold the bacon bits), but the language barrier is not easy to cross, so I gave up. Actually, my favorite part of the meal was watching the Polish newscast on the television in the dining room. The experience was complete when, on our way out, we heard a small child asking his mother if they were going in "Babcia's car".

On the way back we stopped at a courtyard garden nursery. Native and exotic plants lined the sides and center rows of the brick surrounded space. It has only been in the past few years that I have noticed plants or taken any interest in them, but I was fascinated to find many that I had never seen before. The owner/caretaker patiently described their attributes as we browsed. Then I saw a monster plant. No kidding, this beast stood roughly twelve feet tall, and could have starred in *Little Shop of Horrors*. Its enormous, deep green leaves engulfed everything beneath it. Amazed, I asked what kind of plant it was. "Oh, that? Just some weed," he replied casually. I guess I'll never again complain about the weeds in my gardens.

We took a lazy break back at Spencer and Michelle's house. Senator and I drifted between napping and watching the Olympics. Generally I could not care less about any sporting event, but I suppose there is something awe-inspiring about a row of manly European women perched on the edge of a pool, ready to swim feverishly for their countries' honor. I turned to look out the window instead. I scarcely remember the rest of the afternoon passing by.

Saturday night's plan was significantly more tranquil than the previous night's entertainment. Most notably, there would be no punk concerts starring wild senior citizens. Instead, we would walk a few blocks to a local tacqueria, grab some simple Mexican fare, and head back for an early night of hanging out. On the way, we happened to pass a bar/café with outdoor tables. At one of those tables sprawled Eric, the Smarmy Smoker, an acquaintance of our friends.

My apologies to our dear friends if Eric is among their kindred spirits, but we thought the guy was, quite frankly, an ass. Eric, though older than my parents, somehow believed himself to be a chic young New York playboy. His exaggerated gestures only succeeded in making his ridiculous tales even more incredulous. We were from Joliet? Why, yes, he had been there once. He believed it was during the 70s, and he was at a disco, and he had fabulous platform shoes, etc., etc., who cares, etc.. I did not bother to point out that 1.)I do not remember nor care about the 1970s, and 2.)there were no known discos in Joliet fitting his description. I was too busy scooting my chair around the table, awkwardly trying to avoid his stale cigarette smoke, which I swear he trained to chase me. None too soon we parted company from the clown.

When it comes to Mexican food, Senator and I are fairly spoiled. While there are no discos in Joliet, there are many authentic Mexican eateries, and no lack of delicious tortilla and burrito concoctions. We were now eager to try Brooklyn's version of this cuisine, in the form of a new neighborhood restaurant. As we approached, we saw that the place was crowded, traffic buzzing in and out with carry-out orders.

We opted to eat in, so we were seated at a small table in the tiny dining area. The décor was simple, which I took as a good sign. It appeared that they focused only on straightforward, no-nonsense authentic Mexican working-class food. In fact, the waiter plopped down next to us and spent the first five minutes of our relationship telling us how excited they were to be open, and how they had spent five years researching the food to make sure it was prepared exactly as Mexican 'street cuisine' should be. It sounded great, and we all ordered.

After a questionably long time, a few plates trickled our way from the kitchen. The portions were tiny, and they were mixed up. Some of Senator's food was mixed with Michelle's order, while I could not even guess which one was mine. Still, we were game to try different items, so we dealt. Of course, we did make the incorrect assumption that the other half of the food would come as well. Eventually it did, but not together. I could also point out the fact that we never did receive our drinks, but why quibble? Please don't misunderstand, Reader-- as a former waitress I am quite generous in my allowances toward server/kitchen error, but this was a bit much. When it was all said and done, the food was not even as tasty as some of the stuff I make, and I can hardly claim the streets of Mexico as my heritage.

The meal was disappointing, but bumming around with fun friends never is. We walked further, and Michelle declared that we should bring home some tiramisu. We unanimously agreed that we deserved it, and the motion and the tiramisu were carried. We sat on the couch recapping the day, and I was amazed at how quickly this last weekend of my summer was going.

It seemed like there was something special about Saturday, but I couldn't remember what it was. Then it hit me. I had figured out, (probably when I was stalling from writing,) that Saturday marked 100 days that we had traveled during our 5+ years together. I am not sure that it meant anything, but it was a good enough reason for me to take another bite of dessert.

Sunday mornings in New York, according to my careful calculations, are always sunny. Though it may turn to a cloudy sky later in the day, the morning always seems to live up to its name. After sleeping in again, we enjoyed another round of Juice via Michelle's toy. A morning news program was on the television, which we could comfortably see from the deck. The light breeze gave the scene a casual May feeling. In a few days I would face a new crop of teenagers and their numerous individual needs and issues, but for now, they were every bit of the 800 miles away.

I looked over at Senator. He was rotating between playing with one of the dogs and lying on his back soaking up the sun. It was good to see him so content and relaxed. This was the Brooklyn people forget about.

We had not really been paying attention to the news until we heard something about Arches National Park. Having just visited there less than two months before, we sat up and took notice. The reporter went on to state that a massive slab of rock had collapsed from one of the arches, marking the first significant geological event in the park since 1991. How very extraordinary! Fortunately, no one happened to be lining their family up for a vacation photograph underneath it at the time, but this made it official: we cause catastrophes of one sort or another whenever we travel. Senator and I looked at one another, gently nodded, and silently wondered what we should destroy next.

Demolishing eons' worth of rock formations gave us an appetite just in time for brunch. Spencer, our chef-in-residence had prepared frittatas with an assortment of fresh veggies and cheese. The four of us enjoyed the meal and one another's company on the deck. At the opposite end of the patio, their puppy put the final bite on another chew toy.

As a temporary diversion from our lounging, we decided to walk along with our friends as they ran a few errands. (Surely a comfortable walking pace would burn off a weekend's worth of calories.) We turned out onto the main street, which was somewhat quieter than Saturday, but still alive with activity. Michelle ducked in resale shop to unload of few unwanted garments.

We poked around in the basement of another second-hand store. These wonderful old musty basements simultaneously hold the elegant and the tacky. An eighty-year old parlour sofa stood next to a tray of ugly odd pieces of a dinnerware set. When, pray tell, did the 1970s become antique? Not that I am complaining, mind you. I have successfully sold quite a few items from my childhood to other Gen-Xers desperately trying to buy back their own.

We came back upstairs and met Spencer and the dogs on the street. Michelle followed a moment later. On the way back to the house, they decided to stop by a pet store. I forget their initial reason for going inside, but while there, they spied a new chew toy for the puppy. The terry cloth octopus was purple and green, and gave a lusty squeak when squished.

Reading the package, I learned something new. Apparently there is a rating system for how tough pet toys are. Wimpy puppies can get by with a toy that rates 1-4, while the average dog is good with a 5-8. Our friends unanimously agreed that they must have a 10. The clerk assured them that this object was the Craftsman tool of chew toys-- virtually indestructible.

Michelle plunked down the money at once, and we walked outside with the dogs.

The octopus was an instant success. Tokie trotted merrily along, his new best friend dangling from his mouth by a tentacle. Once home, he introduced the octopus to his cage and all of his favorite spots. The magic heightened when he discovered that his pal squeaked as well. All that was missing was The Turtles' *So Happy Together* playing in the background. After wearing himself out with joy, he settled in under the dining room table.

The four of us hung out in the living room, talking and occasionally checking in on the Olympics. I couldn't believe that I was almost slipping into another nap. I was milking this summer break thing for all it was worth. The afternoon was quiet. In fact, the afternoon was very quiet. In fact, the puppy had been exceptionally quiet.

It was Senator who first caught a glimpse of the stream of white cotton batting that lay under the table. He emitted a gasp that made the rest of us look. There sprawled a satisfied puppy, surrounded by little clouds of fluff that once served as the brains and muscle of an unfortunate octopus. The mercilessly decapitated toy choked out its last pathetic squeak, a monster of the great deep no longer. "Number 10 my ass!" intoned Spencer. Either the packaging had lied, or Tokie was one tough puppy. I believe it was a combination of the two. And that, my friends, is why there are no octopi in the East River...

After witnessing the horrors of the short-lived friendship, it was time for another excursion. For the past three days Michelle had been extolling the virtues of her new favorite dessert. If you ever meet Michelle, do not let her slender figure fool you; she is a great connoisseur of sugar. Her latest, greatest discovery was frozen key lime pie on a stick. Of course. Who *wouldn't* visit Brooklyn and think of a tropical dessert served like a Midwest carnival treat? Neither Senator nor I had really given key lime pie much thought in our lives, and neither of us were fans of chocolate, but we were not about to squelch her enthusiasm. Why not give it a go?

Once again we four piled into our friends' car and Spencer drove us to another part of Brooklyn. By the time we arrived it had started to drizzle. *Good, this should weed out some of the competition.* Recently more locals had caught on to the trendy snack. We got out of the car and walked up to the door. The tiny establishment looked like a half-abandoned bait shop along a lonely wharf in Florida. Tropical plants-- don't ask me how-- lined the exterior.

As we filed inside, a few more people squeezed past us on their way out, toting carefully wrapped, impaled concoctions. We stepped into the dark room, approached the counter and ordered four of the strange desserts. I could not help but notice the surplus of flamingo decorations. A moment later we were seated around an umbrella table outside, nibbling bits of paradise.

This was a totally unexpected sensation. Imagine the comfort of a graham cracker crust situated next to a citrus crème, and topped with smooth, rich dark chocolate. I don't mean the crummy milk-chocolate glop that tasteless Americans invented to hold in the guts of their candy bars; this was a bittersweet compliment. Maybe that is why it was so good. It was not too sweet, just decadent. I finished last, perfecting the balance between savoring my pie and eating it before it melted. Now we understood why Michelle was so excited. Someday when I am an older, wiser amateur pastry chef, I may attempt these at home. In the meantime, however, I can only imagine it ending in liquefied choco-lime disaster.

For reasons which currently escape me, we stopped at a speaker store in the neighborhood on the way back. I think Spencer was checking on audio paraphernalia for something or other. It was sort of an odd little store. It's not that I can particularly compare it to other speaker stores, but I wasn't quite sure about the rabbit. On one of the shelves sat a six or eight inch plastic rabbit that held a cigarette, which, if lit, would give the distinct impression that the rabbit was smoking. That is, of course, if one were given to the general assumption that plastic rabbits enjoy a casual smoke while browsing small shops. If only I were furnishing my home in mid- 1980s dorm room...

All afternoon the rain drizzled on, happy to be free from the restrictions of being pent up all Sunday morning. It was a night made for ordering pizza in. With predictable Olympic events playing in the background, we folded big, floppy pieces of pizza over, careful to corral bits of eggplant, tomato and mozzarella. Something soft was touching my bare feet. I peeked under the table to see a leftover piece of fluff from the late octopus.

After dinner we settled in to watch a documentary* about The Rolling Stones, called *Shine a Light*. The film, directed by Martin Scorsese, followed the band predictably, capturing most of a concert performed at the Beacon Theatre in New York. Though certainly entertaining, the historian in me prefers a more candid approach. It was a little too produced, and a little too correct. Perhaps I've been sucked into the dark underworld of bootlegs and 'rare live' recordings, but I would rather view/listen to a forty year old impromptu interview, radio spot, or unruly concert. Still, it delivered what it was supposed to: Jagger's energetic (if tone-deaf) vocals, Richards' staggering and charismatic persona, interjected tripe from Scorsese, and a whole lot of fun.

Fifteen minutes after it ended we were in bed. I lay there quietly and looked out the windows. Tomorrow we would fly home, and I was not sure when we would be back. I drank in the skyline. Then I turned over and looked at Senator. I was suddenly filled with a surge of gratitude for the privilege of

---

*Okay, *rock*umentary, but I hate that term

sharing this with him. My mind wandered to one of the earliest conversations I had ever had with him. He was working in his music department and I popped in to say hello and feed off of his presence, which I always found so calming. All at once I was struck with a vision of us in a grand ballroom, with random, formless couples around us. We were dressed impeccably. Without giving it a thought I blurted out, "Someday, I would very much like to dance with you!" I thought it was an innocent enough proclamation, but Senator later expounded on his theories concerning the depths of intimacy associated with dancing with someone. Apparently the boy was right. I was getting too sentimental for my own good, and I had not even been drinking. I ran my hand along his back and kissed him goodnight.

  Monday morning we woke up and said our good-byes as our friends left for work. Our plan was to hang around the neighborhood until it was time to take a cab to the airport. We did this for a while, but found it much more pleasing to sit on the roof deck and watch a nasty storm roll in from the west. Wicked purple clouds swirled over Midtown Manhattan as the wind kicked up. The dogs took turns surveying the situation.

  Soon the drops came in giant angled splatters. We ran into the house to close the necessary windows. By the time the patio was completely wet, the rain had stopped. We ventured back outside, bringing a few chunks of cheese and crackers along for the show. Once again we perched ourselves opposite Manhattan. Widescreen t.v. indeed. The clouds continued to dance menacingly for an hour or so before settling down.

  The performance was over and it was time to go. I called for a ride from the car company, carefully dialing the correct number. (Oddly, the competition had an almost identical phone number.) We took one last glance around the house, told the dogs good-bye, and bid the octo-carcus a final farewell. It would be quite a while before we traveled again. The 2008 season was over. In fact, to keep my travel addiction in check, I vowed to Senator that we would spend every night at home in our own bed until the holidays came along. Of course, 2009 was just around the corner...

Chapter 5
Song of the South: Early April 2009

"Little darling, it's been a long cold lonely winter..."[*] Well perhaps it was not lonely, but for the eight month travel hiatus of 2008-2009, two out of three definitely applied. Upon returning from New York, Senator and I once again dove head first into work, side projects, and the neverending phenomenon that is downsizing. The fall was spent in sale mode.

A gross overcalculation in optimism led us to believe that it would somehow be worth our while to host a garage sale. What did we have to lose? We would get rid of some junk, enjoy a few good cups of coffee on our little plot of terra firma, observe the local wildlife, and make easy money. Yes, we believed that mid-September, when our town held its annual garage sale extravaganza, would be the perfect time of year weatherwise to tackle such an event. After eight hours of watching the downpour from inside in our tiny garage, we re-evaluated this notion. The single overhead light bulb lamely illuminated 97% of the sale items that we had started with. In the end, we did make enough to buy ourselves a good sized pizza, which was

---

[*]from *Here Comes the Sun*, written by George Harrison

our only goal, but the sales-per-productivity-hours ran somewhere in the $4 range.

Slightly dampened in spirit and quite dampened in clothing, we changed our focus to the next endeavors: two more installments of Daver's Last Record Show. In the years we have been together, I have assisted Senator with about eight record shows. He loads up the car, I tie on my old waitress apron, and together we drive to a banquet hall in Chicago's south suburbs to stand behind a folding table and smile and banter our way into selling off some of his vinyl collection. Each time we drag ourselves out of bed at 4:00am, he swears it is his last show. Then each time we have a blast and come home with more cash than either of us makes in a week, he starts to think that *maybe* he'll do one more show.

With the record shows over, we were on to the holidays, and winter was in full swing. I actually do love winter, but this year it came screaming in mercilessly. It seemed that every few days we rotated between bitter driving winds, dangerous ice storms, and debilitating blizzards. The new year then added the bonus of constant sub-zero temperatures. No, I mean *sub-zero* as in getting to zero would have felt like a balmy spring day. It was brutal, and my yen to travel had been suppressed entirely too long.

By late January, I had an outlined plan. There were only six states that we had not been to together, and four of them were located in the Deep South. *Just how deep is 'Deep'?* I wondered. We could follow I-55 right down the Mississippi River, exploring that mysterious land that evokes so many images: struggles for equality, southern hospitality, feisty independence, and, of course, the cradle of our musical heritage. To put it politely, I was curious to explore unfamiliar territory. To put it blatantly, I was curious to see if I would be able to shake the one stereotype I am guilty of holding-- that of the southern hick. Race, gender, age, and looks have never been an issue with me, but for some reason-- and I am not proud to admit this-- I hear a southern accent and immediately think the person is less educated, culturally backward, and planning his/her next BBQ and beer binge. Forgive me, Lord.

Of course, battling social misconceptions was not the only reason for choosing the South. Senator had spent a significant portion of the winter engrossed in the history of the early independent record labels. The most famous of these, Sun Studio, just happened to be on the way. We would also trace several beloved musical genres back to their roots. Blues, country, some forms of jazz, and even hip-twitchin' rock 'n' roll were born in the Mississippi River Valley*. Throw in a few historical and literary sites for good measure, and we had one packed week of touring ahead of us.

Oh, yes. I almost forgot. There was also the objective of New Orleans, take two. If you have read any chapters in any of my books, you may have noticed that disaster often surrounds our vacations in one form or another. The first time we attempted to go to New Orleans, Katrina beat us to it. Two and a half years later, New Orleans seemed to be back in the full swing of 'big easiness'.

On a sunny Saturday morning that still hinted of winter, we began our journey, heading south through our bedraggled state of Illinois. During the previous months, political scandal and another corrupt governor had all but bankrupted the land of Honest Abe. The public facilities accurately reflected this. When I couldn't hold it until Missouri, we pulled off the interstate to an Illinois rest area.

In the bathroom stall, I balanced clumsily on a broken seat. To my left was a pathetic roll of single-ply toilet paper (emphasis on *paper*). To my right, water trickled heavily from a

---

*Despite clinging to the image for public relations purposes, Chicago is, at best, *a* home of the blues-- not *the* home of the blues.

busted pipe. I finished my business, vowed never to pee at an Illinois rest area again, and stepped out to wash my hands. Sink #1 did not work. Neither did sink #2. Feeling like the victim of a con man taunting me to find the ball under the cup, I tried sink #3. Cold water spurted out haphazardly. I didn't dare hope that the hand dryer worked; that's why God invented jeans, anyway.

The one convenience of southern Illinois is its national public radio access. Looking for a few good laughs from *Car Talk*, we found Click and Clack on no less than six stations. If you flipped between them fast enough, you could almost hear the snorts in stereo. An hour of semi-useful automotive advice later, we were in St. Louis.

While it is somewhat inspiring to see the St. Louis Arch from a distance, it is actually not that impressive when you come closer to it. In fact, its stark, steely exterior makes it look just industrious enough to be moved to the Illinois side of the Mississippi River. We efficiently fever-merged around the bend, crossing the river on the overworked bridge by Busch Stadium. Remembering our last experience with Missouri drivers, Senator stepped up his best defensive driving skills. Thankfully, the drive was uneventful and quick. An hour before we anticipated, we were in Memphis.

Most of what we sought in Memphis was downtown, cheap parking included. Just two blocks from Beale Street we paid our five bucks, parked Trucky, and walked toward the music. This is where my first illusion about the South was shattered. Unfortunately, it had been a positive one. Here, where blues and 1950s rock 'n' roll were king, I expected to hear gritty tributes to soulful music pouring out of clubs onto the crammed streets. Instead, we were treated to a melange of average bar cover bands with a penchant for classic rock-- and not even southern classic rock. How very disappointing. Where were the eighty-year old men who played guitar with the skill and melancholy tenderness that only a lifetime of hardship can produce? Not on Beale Street, certainly.

Perhaps I had just overromanticized it. If these characters still exist, they are more likely playing in the neighborhoods like the one we drove through on a side trip. In these areas, so prevalent in Memphis, children played and fought on the dilapidated porches. Dirty laundry hung on the clotheslines like an afterthought in decorating the yard. Stray dogs barked, bared teeth, and went back to sleep at their owners' feet. Aimless characters considered their agenda for the day (or not), while tired women tried to keep up with endless chores. When two pale Yankees drove by, they all seemed to stare in unison.

My other objective on that evening was Schwab's Dry Goods store. Operating continuously since 1876, Schwab's is a very large general store gone wild. While the building and display cases are original, it now packs in throngs of tourists in search of your typical crappy Chinese souvenirs, trinkets, and shirts.

Having exhausted the main stretch of Beale Street in roughly fifteen minutes, we drove a few miles to find a hotel in a much quieter corner of town. Next door was a local tavern, boldly advertising the best pizza in Memphis. It was a smoke-free establishment with a few friendly-looking permanent patrons hanging around, so we went in. I strained my ears to decipher the strong Tennessee accent as we ordered. Then we waited.

We were not in any hurry, but service was slow. We would quickly realize that slow to us was right on time in the South. This seemed to be the case everywhere we went. On vacation, it was charming. In the real world, Senator and I would be crawling the walls if we had coworkers who moved at that pace.

The other 'tradition' we noticed in many places was the requirement of a photo i.d. to use a credit card. I suppose that it is a good idea. Of course, it was also a guarantee that I would always pull out the wrong credit card/i.d. combination from my purse.*

Saturday night in a town known for its music and entertainment history does not necessarily translate to a late night adventure. In our case, the most appealing thing to do was go back to the hotel, get comfortable, and explore the cable options. We learned that there were a lot of news commentary channels. We learned that the Memphis local forecast on the Weather Channel has pretty rockin' music. *Maybe that should be on Beale Street.* We also learned that not much else was available telewise. Thus, Reader, you understand how it came to be that we were sucked into a 1960s Lawrence Welk rerun.

Before you snap this book closed in disgust, consider the following points: 1.)It officially fell into the category of music research when Senator discovered that all of the songs were pre-taped; 2.)I learned to fully appreciate the fact that I was born long after beehive hairdos and polyester skirts in fruit tones had seen their glory days; and 3.)Welk proved that an entire prime time production can be staged with only a few cardboard cutouts as props. Get the actors to stand behind them and wink knowingly, and the audience will be swept into the fantasy, believing that the performers are, in fact, riding in a real bus/plane/train.

Welk was a wild Saturday night, but we still managed to get up early Sunday. Our first stop was Sam Phillips' Recording Company. When he moved from Sun Record Company in 1960, Sam relocated to this larger facility just a few blocks away. The exterior of the building and the mod logo on the front kept the era alive. The tiny parking lot had only a Cadillac limousine with a flat tire that did not seem to concern anybody. Perhaps it

---

*This prompted a dumb joke or two from cashiers about Senator not "looking like a Wendy".

belonged to one of the residents of the apartment building to the rear, where impressive graffiti could be seen through the razor wire. No one stirred on this cool, quiet morning, which was probably a good thing. We snapped a picture and left.

In moments we were the first people to arrive at Sun Studio. Lawrence Welk notwithstanding, now the trip was really getting good! We entered what looked like a small malt shop/gift shop and shuffled together as the room quickly filled up. A sweet college age girl then led us upstairs to a museum, where echoes of the past and a few rare recordings came to life. From Elvis to Carl Perkins, to Howlin' Wolf, to Johnny Cash, stories of life-changing recording sessions with Sam Phillips were told. Black and white, the blues, and eventually rock 'n' roll, came out of the small studio room at 706 Union Street. Today, it remains remarkably unchanged, still housing its original sound absorption panels and a microphone Elvis used. Shhh, listen...

We continued our musical tour at the Memphis Rock and Soul Museum. Sponsored by the Smithsonian Institute, the museum is a great multimedia crash course in how the culture of Memphis shaped its unique sound. After watching the introductory video, one of the employees passed out headphones and hand held electronic boxes. I promptly dropped mine, yanking the cord out of the socket, and landing the box on the floor with a clunk. Oops. I resituated and we walked into the first gallery.

This is where the brilliance comes in. At each of the exhibits, there was the traditional written information, but there was also a number listed. If you punched the number into the box, you heard sound bites from actual artist interviews and radio broadcasts. It was like being let loose to run through a portion of history with those who made it as your guides.

I hope all museums go to this system eventually. Of course, it is not perfect, though. The danger of absentmindedly walking into someone while engrossed in your own world is still present, and it makes for a quiet date between a couple. I suppose, too, it could be difficult to dig up interviews with prehistoric characters if the Field Museum installed this technology. It could be interesting, though...

We completed our rounds and left the museum, stepping out into glaring sun and intense winds-- neither of which were helping Senator's rapidly growing headache. He decided to medicate it with some coffee. If you want to open a business on Beale Street with no competition, apparently you should open a café, because they do not exist. We ducked into a restaurant and bought a cup to go. When the waitress handed Senator a plastic cup of hot coffee, we knew this simple request was going to be more challenging than we had imagined. Eight feet from the restaurant's entrance, he dropped the softening cup into the trash. Admitting defeat, we trudged to the Starbucks in the next block.

All the while I had been urging haste because we had a reservation for a guitar factory tour at Gibson soon afterward. Their website had strongly recommended reservations, and I obediently complied. Of course, when I called to reserve a time, I neglected to figure in that I was reserving a *southern* time.[*] There was no danger of us being late. About ten minutes after the scheduled start time, with just a few other couples, our tour began.

To fully appreciate the Gibson Guitar Factory tour, you have to have a guide like the one we had. He was about thirty years old, heavyset, with long, frizzy hair, a scraggly beard, and a marvelously sarcastic dry humor. Like a group of school children, we marched through the plant, looking but not

---

[*]To convert, you have to take the Central Time Zone and average it with the Mountain Time Zone, adding five minutes for every degree of latitude south of the Mason Dixon Line.

touching. Racks of naked guitar bodies sat, patiently awaiting the next step in their assembly. He noted that different types of woods were used for different lengths of sustain of the sound.

We then saw the press that cuts the signature curved top of a Gibson guitar, which our guide noted was the same shape as an "old-timey moustache". He held the neck up so that the top aligned with his upper lip to demonstrate. *Hhmmm, can't argue with that comparison.* We filed past the paint and glaze stalls, and into the area where workers painstakingly scrape the edges of the guitars for the cosmetic detailing. I imagine that job gets old after about ten minutes.

Our guide concluded the tour by asking if there were any questions about the "vast awesomeness that has unfolded before you". A hand raised in the back.

"What do you do with the guitars that don't meet your quality standards after they're made?" asked one man.

"We repackage them and send them to Fender to sell," he replied, without missing a beat. He then showed us to the gift shop, where, rather than the usual assortment of plastic junk, the price tags ranged in the thousands for your very own Gibson guitar. I opted for a stunning black and silver model... and then realized I didn't have the extra few grand cash on me that day.

We left Gibson and walked the block back to the car. The only Memphis stop remaining was Stax. Stax was the record label that promoted American soul music and entertainment, from Isaac Hayes to Bill Cosby. We had not originally intended to go, but Senator read about a record shop there, so with a Memphis street map in my lap, I navigated us toward the address.

Moments later we were out of the downtown area and into the hood. The area was not looking too promising in the way of attractions, but soon we came to a brightly colored entrance for the Stax Museum. In back we found four empty police cars, and parked Trucky next to them. We joined hands and walked to the front, looking comically out of place. Bypassing the museum, we headed directly to the record shop, which turned out to be nothing more than a glorified gift shop. Booo. At least the ride had been interesting.

We arrived back at our hotel in time to go swimming before dinner. For the most part we had the pool to ourselves, which was nice, but it also highlighted the fact that we were not exactly in Olympic shape. Senator panted a bit. I took frequent breaks between swimming laps across the short side of the pool. Yes, I know that you are not supposed to swim it that way, but I refuse to swim in water that is deeper than me, and at 5'1", this limits one's options considerably.

We pushed hard for a while longer and then got out of the pool. I decided that we weren't exhausted from the workout, just weak from hunger after not eating much all day. It sounded better, anyway. We dried ourselves as much as possible and dripped our way back to our room. *Well, what did they expect when they give skimpy little towels to people with as much hair as us?*

While getting ready for dinner we mechanically turned on the Weather Channel. More wind, more unseasonably cool temperatures. It sounded like the trend we had witnessed for months in the Midwest. We must have brought it with us.

Senator flipped over to the news. On vacation we are exposed to more news than we generally are at home, due to the fact that we have little leisure time and no television service at home. The extra knowledge about the world is not necessarily a good thing. For example, in the week that we were gone, we learned that North Korea had broken its promise by launching a 'satellite'. The rest of the world was fairly certain it was testing missile range. In Italy, over 100 people had died in an earthquake. Then there was the nut in Seattle who had killed his five children to spite his ex. Throughout the United States, police officers had experienced more casualties than usual, and a U.S.

ship captain was being held hostage by Somali pirates.* It briefly occurred to me that we had also arrived in Memphis on the anniversary of Dr. Martin Luther King's assassination. Maybe our tendency toward vacation mayhem had now expanded to a global level.

No, we agreed that there was nothing to be gained by watching the news on vacation. We said a prayer for all of those facing tragedy, and switched off the television to live in the past for a week. Leaving the hotel, we drove around in search of something interesting to eat. It was encouraging to learn that parts of Memphis really were beautiful. We turned into a neighborhood with stately old homes and colorful blooming gardens. At home, everything that would be green was still in bare, hibernation mode. The fitting end of our spontaneous turn was an inviting Indian restaurant. Remember, I said "interesting", not necessarily local. Although, some of the vegetables were deep fried, so maybe it was southern Indian cuisine.

Monday morning we woke up ready to hit the road again. The sky was gray and Memphis had served its purpose. Now we were heading into Mississippi, a state I had somehow managed to miss my entire life, most likely because it is not on the way to anywhere else.

We were in the Deep South now; there was no turning back. For having a reputation as such a poor state, everywhere we went in Mississippi was very attractive and well maintained. This was evidenced by their rest areas, which were spotless, completely updated, and put Illinois' to shame. The only drawback about traveling along I-55 in the Magnolia State is the roller coaster effect of some of the roads. They are smoothly

---

*Captain Richard Phillips was miraculously rescued the next week, on Easter Sunday, when Navy Seals outwitted the four pirates, killing three of them, and arresting the fourth. U.S.A.! U.S.A.!

paved, but they roll up and down like waves for miles at a time. You may wish to cross it off your list of possible trips if you get sea sick easily.

When we got down to Jackson, we changed to I-20 toward Vicksburg. Oh, Vicksburg, where do we begin? During the Civil War, Vicksburg stood as the last holdout against the damned Yankees breaking through the lines on the Mississippi. Eventually, a siege from two different directions forced the city's surrender. Sadly, it fell simultaneously with Gettysburg, decidedly giving the North the edge it would need to eventually win the war.

On this particular spring day, though, the Vicksburg National Battlefield was under the siege of a boy scout troop. Upon leaving the introductory video theatre, we met a surprise attack. Each was armed with a penny whistle, which he blew mercilessly. This time, the Yankees retreated back to their car, eager to escape the high-pitched barrage.

The battlefield features a 16-mile loop drive that takes you back into the woods and up into the hills, snaking around monuments the entire way. Battle lines for Union and Confederate soldiers are also outlined. It is a serene and scenic drive, especially pleasant in the spring. The highlight of the drive, without question, is the Union ironclad gunboat, *Cairo*.

One moment you are winding around memorials, and the next moment you curve around to find the entire structure standing imposingly at the foot of a hill. In 1862, *Cairo* ran interference to destroy Confederate batteries, until it was sunk by an amazingly early version of a mine. Surprisingly, artifacts and the ship itself survived a century underwater before being resurrected in the 1960s. The salvaged wreck is in excellent shape, and it is a rare treat for a Civil War historian to be staring down a battleship from the era. It is hard enough to find buildings that have survived the time period well, let alone a vehicle. Even if you are not into military history, it would be worth the trip off the beaten path through Mississippi to see this unique relic.

Even at a leisurely pace, we were running ahead of schedule. By late afternoon we were already to the Louisiana state line. We decided to drive all the way to New Orleans instead of waiting until the morning. We had a hotel reservation for the next night, but I wasn't sure we would be able to find a room for that night on such short notice. The decision was made to employ the road tripper's strategy of stopping at the state line welcome center.

We pulled into the parking lot in front of the neat, white-washed building. Inside, two jolly ladies were lamenting the fact that between wireless internet connections and GPS systems, no one bothers to ask them anything anymore. "They just stop for the free coffee!" pronounced one. We looked to the complementary coffee station across the room. They were right. I vowed not to let their expertise go to waste. Senator gathered pamphlets of attractions and street maps. I browsed the lodging information. There, in the very front, I spied an advertisement for the hotel we would be staying in the next night. It advertised $50 rooms for a same-night reservation. The Hotel St. Marie was considered a splurge on this trip, and I could not imagine they would have any room that cheap. Pamphlet in hand, I approached the counter.

"I have a question," I began. I had their instant attention. "Is this an actual promotion, because this is the hotel we are staying in tomorrow night anyway, and it would be great to add tonight as well. What's the catch?"

"Actually, you can *only* get that promotional rate through us," she beamed proudly. "You would have to make a reservation for tonight, and then mention us," she explained.

"Thank you!" we chimed in unison. I decided to play it up just a bit. "I'm so glad we stopped here! You guys-- I mean y'all-- have been such a help!"

We went back to the car and I fumbled with the cell phone to call the phone number. Amazing. There was reception where I needed it, and a full battery to boot. Things were coming together. When the receptionist answered the phone, I explained the deal, mentioning that I was at the welcome center right then, for added effect. She seemed uninterested as she silently clicked along on her keyboard. A pause. As I had no plan B, the suspense was mounting. "Well, I do have one room left, but it's a balcony suite." I figured my promotional scam was a bust, but it couldn't hurt to ask. "Would you honor this price if I book the suite?" I ventured.

"Yes, we can do that." She sounded more bored than anything.

"I'll take it!" I rattled off my credit card number, and the deal was done. I still can't figure out why she sounded apologetic when she told me that only a balcony suite was available. Maybe she was regretting the fact that their elegant room was only bringing in the price of a flea bag hotel.

Having secured lodging, we drove on with purpose. About a half hour outside the city, the highway became a sort of elevated swamp trail. Marshy waters sat stagnant to the left, the right, and beneath us. Occasionally we could see a shack floating on a few planks where land and water meshed. I fail to see the romance in a swamp. Unless you are fortunate enough to see an alligator, which we did not, I think of swamps as massive breeding grounds for mosquitoes, the scourge of all humanity.

We came to the bottom of the country and joined interstate I-10 through New Orleans. We scanned the horizon on either side, but never really noticed any leftover hurricane damage. I am not saying it is not present, but one cannot see it as easily as one might think. The highway curved, we took our exit, and in a few blocks we were in the French Quarter.

Oh. I guess I expected some sort of transition. In the rear view mirror was a typical urban street scene with a gas station, some businesses, and stop lights. Before us sprawled a transformed world that looked like nothing else I had ever seen in the United States. Black lanterns perched on the corners, supporting antique street signs written in French. Small shops and eateries hung their signs from the bottoms of balconies that ran around the second stories of buildings. Colorful exteriors were complemented by the tropical plants that grew through black iron scroll work that blended Spanish architecture with French mansard roof lines. The street was alive-- not wild-- just alive. Music poured out of a few directions, and casual locals and excited tourists opened full-length shutters to let the humid breeze in.

The Hotel St. Marie is conveniently situated at the corner of Bourbon and Toulouse Streets. More importantly, it has its own parking deck. Well hidden to protect the integrity of the architecture, the on-site parking was a more important feature than we realized. In the French Quarter, unless you have a resident permit, there is no parking. I do not mean "no parking" as in you might be able to find a spot if it's the off season, or if you can cleverly maneuver your vehicle into imaginative crevices. There is simply no parking allowed in the entire district. This would not be such a problem, except for the fact that hoteliers and travel guides advise that you do not venture too far out of the area on foot. So if you go to the French Quarter, find a hotel that has a deck and save yourself a headache.

We dropped off the car and stepped up to the front desk. A preppy-looking thirty-something greeted us. I explained that we had two different reservations, and that we would be doing a room change for the following night. He assured me that it was not a problem, but he also felt the need to mention the irregularity of it three or four times. *It's okay, Pal. I'm sure you can handle it. I'll bet they don't give those navy blazers out to just anyone.*

The matter being settled, he handed us the key to our room. Wow, it was an actual key. The heavy brass key unlocked a real lock, with no beeps, green flashes, or Dominoes Pizza advertisements involved. The room was lovely. Our long shutters opened to a verandah overlooking Toulouse, just far enough away from Bourbon Street to get a good night's rest. In the bathroom were samples of aromatic French milled soaps. God bless those Louisiana welcome center ladies.

We regrouped, consulted the travel book on the table, and plotted our brief stay. Hhmmm. We could see some sites around the neighborhood, or go vampire hunting in the outlying areas. No thanks on the latter. As much as I am a true Goth kid at heart, the Hollywood undead sensationalism doesn't do it for me. I'll leave that to the Stephanie Meyer crowd.

The book and notes and pamphlets were for the next day. Tonight, the only thing on the agenda was to walk around and absorb. We stepped out the front doors of the hotel and turned left toward Bourbon Street. The wind snapped steadily. By reputation, I expected Bourbon to be an all night, somewhat uncontrolled party, so it was a pleasant surprise to find people laughing, dancing, and having a good time without acting like maniacs. Police were a noticeable presence, though their relaxed nature and smiling nods to tourists made them seem more like public relations advocates.

A street band played jazz while a small crowd gathered. Little did we know that it would be some of the only live jazz we heard in New Orleans. Sadly, the music that spilled into the streets from the venues that lined Bourbon Street was pretty much rock, classic rock, or bad lounge rock. Where was the bayou music? What about the zydeco?* We could have stayed in

---

*The answer to that question was: only out of a cd player in one of the shops. Sad, but true.

Chicago to hear this. Apparently they were playing to their tourists, their bread and butter, who all looked to be 30+.

We continued on, looking for a bite to eat. On Decatur, we came to a small restaurant decorated in an angel theme, New Orleans style. The angels in the murals floated around brightly painted clouds, with a Creole flair. Beads hung on every available hook or post. As in other places in the South, service was not rushed. When our melty veggie sandwiches did arrive, they were delicious. No, Reader, vegetarians do not eat seafood-- no gumbo, no shrimp scampi, no lobster bisque. Do not pity us, though. The food was unbelievable! Spinach, tomato, and a garlicky warm hummus on toasted French rolls went down easily.

We finished faster than the waiter anticipated. I think our northern rate of consuming a meal could probably take a few tips from the South. Now it was time to pretend we were walking off the calories. We marched back down Decatur and snaked our way up and down the rest of the French Quarter.

Royal Street lives up to its name. Outrageously expensive boutiques line the street, with window displays that rival Manhattan. Gorgeous European furniture and artistic pieces are graciously arranged to highlight the fact that they are probably worth more than my entire home. Horse-drawn carriages clomping down the street add to the effect. If it's French, unaffordable, and something you probably don't need, you can find it on Royal.

We continued to meander our way around Chartres, and the 'other' half of Bourbon, before arriving back at our hotel. Apparently, if you go far enough south on Bourbon, you enter the Naked District. At least, on a Monday night anyway, the nudity was confined to behind the doors of clubs, and not on the street. Here reside such classy establishments as Larry Flynt's Hustler Club. You can also find other clubs that advertise girls, barely legal girls, girls who like other girls, and a few boys who like other boys. We pivoted back to the other half of Bourbon--the part reserved for people who don't have to pay to the see someone naked. Before we realized it, we were back in our room, dozing off to the sounds of distant tunes.

No matter how nice a hotel room is, you never sleep as well as when you are in your own bed. Early Tuesday morning we awoke to voices on the street below, and the sound of large trucks. *It must be garbage day.* I rolled over and dozed off until I heard more trucks.

It was about time to get up anyway, so I got out of bed and cracked open the shutter to peer outside. On the street below were water trucks making their usual rounds. All of the streets in the French Quarter get sprayed down with soapy water every morning. I'll let you use your imagination here to supply any reasons for why this practice came to be. Now, with a clean New Orleans sparkling beneath our feet, it was time to set out.

Café du Monde was our first stop. If you are unfamiliar with it, this particular café bears the distinction of being the oldest coffee shop in the United States, caffeinating those in need since 1870. Take that Seattle. They are also famous for supplying the French Quarter with its quota of *beignets*, a sort of square, puffy French doughnut doused with powdered sugar. Every morning, the outdoor café and take-out windows fill up with patrons anxious to taste yet another exotic version of the magical combination of fat and sugar.[*]

We sat in the sun and finished our beignets, working equally hard to keep our wind-whipped hair out of our coffee and our mouths. Across the street sat Jackson Square. Roaming the path through the gardens leads you to the steps of St. Louis Cathedral, the oldest Catholic Cathedral in the United States,

---

[*]Beignets are tasty, but we are still partial to Native American fry bread when it comes to this category.

absolving those in need since 1718. Ergo, if you like old Catholics and old coffee, this is the place to be.

The doors to the church were unlocked, so we invited ourselves in. Candles flickered when the door opened, letting in the chilly breeze that still hovered over half of the country. Mass was taking place, so we did not enter the sanctuary. Instead, we walked through the foyer, making a mental note to stop back later. Stop back for what, you ask? For the gift shop, of course! Don't knock it; if your church was almost 300 years old, you would have one, too.

We marched through more of the French Quarter, changing sides of the street to follow the sun's warmth. A record store and book store later, we had wasted another hour. The record store yielded Senator a cd of Cosimo Matassa recordings that he had been interested in. Matassa lived in the area and had the epiphany that no one was recording the rhythm and blues greats like Fats Domino and Little Richard, so he stepped up to the board. The book store yielded me the opportunity to stand in what had served as a brief residence of William Faulkner. Nothing in the place suggested him, though. I was especially annoyed that the owners allowed a dog to roam the inside. Ggrrr!* I left empty-handed, but looking forward to visiting Faulkner's *real* home in northern Mississippi.

One of the funny things about the French Quarter is that, though it is less than a mile square, there are doubles of some shops and restaurants. I guess they want to make sure that they get your business, even if you are too lazy to walk four blocks to their twin. Even among different stores, the layout is basically the same. At the front are the shirts with clever sayings. My personal favorite read, "I went to New Orleans during Katrina and all I got was this lousy television, dvd player, stereo..."

Beyond the shirts are the fake voodoo altars, with

---

*My comment; not the dog's.

115

enticing warnings to stand back and keep your hands to yourself, as though any religious iconography that they believed in would really be out front for the tourists. At the back end of the store you can browse other New Orleans essentials, from rubber alligators to powdered beignet mix, all while experiencing the distinct scent of clove cigarettes and the apparently timeless tunes of Fleetwood Mac. We never did understand why, but we heard far more than our fair share of Fleetwood Mac songs while in New Orleans. Who knows-- maybe Stevie Nicks was a closet voodoo priestess.

It delighted me, then, when we stumbled upon the Jean LaFitte museum. Situated in what looks like a storefront, it was a great little interpretive center, from the heart of the National Park Service to you. Inside the displays were fairly basic, but they gave an accurate picture of the history of the French culture in southeastern Louisiana. We learned that the word 'Creole' originally referred to a Louisiana native, regardless of ethnicity. After getting a few tips on visiting local cemeteries, we ventured back out into the restless wind.

Sufficient time had passed, so we returned to Catholic Central to see if the church was open. We were just in time to see a procession pour out of the doors, including the bishop and dozens of priests in white robes. It was a solemn moment of blessing the onlookers, yet I couldn't help but smile when the wind kicked up, sending vestments billowing out like sails from human masts. A quick glance out of the corner of my eye confirmed that Senator found it just as funny as I did. Containing ourselves, we waited for the group to move out before entering the sanctuary.

Inside, the cathedral reminded me of a few of the beautiful churches in Joliet. An oversized, ornate crucifix stood above the altar, and the room was washed with soft but bright light. The major difference, however, were the historical artifacts from the church's early days. The gift shop, which had finally opened, sold all things Catholic, from rosaries to saints-on-chains to plastic bottles. Senator purchased a pair of these for his mother and aunt. "What are those?" I asked in my Protestant naivete.

"Holy water."

"They *sell* holy water in the gift shop?! Isn't that illegal or something?"

"No," he calmly continued, "they sell empty bottles with the cathedral's picture on it and you have to go fill it up yourself." Fascinated, I had to see how this worked. Like a faithful sidekick, I followed him up to one of the side nooks near the front of the sanctuary. I watched in curiosity as he filled the bottles from what looked like a regular water cooler. *No kiddin'?* So that was all it took to acquire holy water from the oldest cathedral in the U.S.. Either that, or we just got two bottles full of the priests' Hinckley and Schmitt.

By now we were ready to check back into our hotel. We had covered the entire French Quarter several times over, and some kick-back time sounded good. Along the way, a shopkeeper trying to hawk something or other yelled for Senator's attention as we passed by, adding that it would make a great gift for "your daughter". We laughed as we kept walking. I wonder what the guy thought when he saw my arm around Senator's waist, with my hand tucked neatly in his jeans pocket.

In our smaller, more expensive room, I flounced on the bed, surrounding myself with a mountain of pillows. Senator leafed through the insert in his new cd. "Where is Dauphine Street?" he asked abruptly.

I laughed. "Look out the window. It just happens to be right below us! Why do you want to know that?"

"It says here that Cosimo Matassa sometimes hangs out in their family-owned deli on Dauphine."

"You're kidding! What are the odds of that? That address is only about four blocks away." Thus, Senator set out on his research mission a few minutes later. I dozed in the pillow mountain.

Unfortunately, Cosimo Matassa, who played such an integral role in preserving the work of some of rhythm and blues' pioneers, is a bit of an enigma. The girl at the deli played dumb when asked about him. Later, she changed her reply to say that he would be in around noon the next day. A desk attendant at our hotel also seemed baffled by the same question, but then quickly brushed by the fact that he was associated with the deli down the street. Even stopping back the next day yielded a different story about Matassa, claiming that he usually comes in the evenings. One employee suggested that he stayed home more now because his wife was ill. For this New Orleans trip, anyway, we closed the interview before it ever began. Perhaps another time, Cosimo...

Disappointment on top of miles of walking equals hunger. We set out again in search of another vegetarian creation. At the opposite end of the quarter, we found it in a tiny bar and grill. The food was great, and the host/waiter was even better. His easy going nature concealed witty retorts. When I asked for a new fork because I noticed something small stuck to mine, he exchanged it with, "Oh yeah. We can't have that. We don't *give* food away here." He did not even break a smile. *Wow, he's good.*

Then came the ordering process. As a vegetarian, you quickly learn that simply not ordering a meat entree does not guarantee a vegetarian dish. Bacon bits are sneaked into salads. Lard can violate a perfectly good plate of beans. When we asked if there was any meat in any part of what we ordered, he delivered the greatest crack at vegetarians we have heard yet. "No, there's no bacon or anything, but the way we look at it, if God didn't want us to eat pigs, he wouldna' made 'em out of food." How could one argue with that logic?

We strolled the ten blocks or so toward the evening's entertainment. The night before we had stumbled upon Preservation Hall, a venue that hosted live jazz played by locals who knew what they were doing. The atmosphere was inviting-- another old building with lots of wood and warmth-- so we decided to check it out. There was no cover charge, but there was a one drink per set minimum. I joked that a set probably lasted ten minutes.

The band started with the fun and energy I had been anticipating. We were enjoying ourselves. I sipped my coffee, held Senator's hand, and sat back to take in a long night of Fleetwood Mac-free music. Just then I smelled smoke. I looked over and sure enough, some fool was lighting up under the 'no smoking' sign. For the past year we had reveled in Illinois' ban on smoking inside all public places. Louisiana did not have this restriction, but one of the things that attracted us to this club was the smoke free environment. I knew I would hate the rest of the night if my hair and clothes reeked of cigarettes, so I decided to speak up. I sauntered up to the manager and said, in my best Big Easy casual voice, "So there *is* smoking in here?" I glanced toward the sign in case he had forgotten.

"Oh, you can smoke *cigarettes*, just not cigars or cloves." *Oh, well, in that case...* This was definitely not a case of 'when in Rome'. A moment later we had tipped our waitress, and we were back out in the street. The funny part is, we were not really that disappointed. I guess we had gotten into the routine of getting in early, getting comfortable, and watching mindless t.v.. Sometimes that's the only definition of vacation you need. I don't really remember falling asleep, but the next thing I knew, it was morning. Again the streets were glistening with the soapy water that erased the night. Before leaving New Orleans we had one more stop to make. Just outside the French Quarter was Lafayette Cemetery, one of the city's oldest graveyards.

Due to its position at sea level (and below, in some sections), New Orleans can not bury its dead, but must entomb them above ground. Otherwise, Aunt Mabel could float down to some other family's plot, creating scads of inheritance fights. The drawback to so many beautiful stone mausoleums lined up in a quiet park is that it makes an ideal setting for nefarious characters-- and I don't mean ghosts-- to perform their evil deeds. Because of this, tourists are urged to go in groups when visiting St. Louis Cemetery, which (in)conveniently, is located in a high-crime ghetto.

Not wanting to join a tour and listen to someone else's interpretation, we set out on our own. Not wanting to get mugged or worse, we chose Lafayette Cemetery over St. Louis. I checked my map and saw that we just needed to go a few blocks away, then onto Canal Street to St. Charles Boulevard. This should have been simple, but we went twenty blocks out of our way on Canal. Returning to our original starting point, I saw a street sign for St. Charles. It was merely the other name for the same street on which we had started.

The street names all changed at Canal. Of course. Why would the names of major streets be consistent? And why would anyone bother with something so trifling as a map that showed both names? I will end my rant here, Reader, but I maintain that the world would be a friendlier place if towns and cities across it left their Elm Streets intact, without changing them to Oaks, Maples, or Mains along the way.

Before arriving at our cemetery, we passed a different, newer one. Senator graciously neglected to ask the obvious question of why we could not just explore *that* one. He knows me too well. Patiently, he drove on until we reached a lovely street of lush gardens. Parking was easy, free, and close to the entrance of Lafayette.

Other couples wandered the tombs, untroubled by criminals. Row after row of crumbling, cold, stone residences filled the acreage. I was thrilled. The crowded plots held people from the past two centuries. Some had suffered diseases that took them at an early age. Others lived as long as any man or woman of our time could expect to live. I did not look for any famous people's graves; celebrity never impresses me. I just experience my moment of tranquility and beauty, and I am happy. In fact, the first time Senator and I were alone together, we were in a graveyard. I guess I'm just a sucker for romance.

It was time to leave New Orleans. My curiosity about the place was satisfied, and going there had temporarily quenched my desire to see Europe. We followed the interstate out of Louisiana and along the Gulf Coast of Mississippi. We never did see any hurricane damage.

What we did see was a rest area in Mississippi that is conjoined with a rocket test site visitor center. I did not know that anything like that existed in areas other than the West. It seemed we were near something related to the military, because during the next hour we saw a huge cargo plane. Then later, while on I-65, a fighter jet flew over the highway.

We had passed the furthest point of our trip, which meant we were officially on our way home. We continued to make excellent time toward Montgomery, so there was no hesitation when we saw the unadorned brown sign advertising Hank Williams' Boyhood Home. How could we pass that up? We had actually planned to stop at the Hank Williams Museum in Montgomery, so we figured this would be a sort of preview.

Turning off of the exit took us down a nearly empty road. A short sign pointed the way to the home. Now we were driving in a neighborhood that could have fit comfortably in any small, middle-class town. Soon we saw the white house with its sprawling front porch. It was less than one hour until closing time, but we were warmly welcomed.

Never underestimate the resource power of a senior volunteer at an underappreciated historical site. As we paced through the rooms checking out family furnishings and local Hank Williams memorabilia, our guided offered juicy tidbits about Hank's health, wealth, wives, career, and brief life. If you can not interview a source directly, forget reading a sterile biography. Instead, talk with an older person who knows somebody who knew the subject. Of course, the story is likely to be biased in favor of the hero, as our lady's undoubtedly was, but your imagination will appreciate it.

Thanking our hostess, we started out the door. I think she enjoyed it as much as we did. I hope so. We were alert and motivated, and we could make Montgomery by evening, so Senator drove on with purpose.

Rush hour traffic was kind of hairy, but going a few miles out of our way brought us out of the crowd. We checked into a modest hotel and sought out a nearby Mexican restaurant. The place was very busy on a Wednesday night, which is always a good sign. Several yards away from the door, we parked Trucky and got out.

"Hey, look at that," I pointed. "There's an African market next door." Having never been inside a market that did not hail from North American or European roots, I deemed it necessary to shop there. Senator obliged, probably not because he felt any pressing need to stock up on exotic fare.

The selection inside was actually quite weak. One uninterested woman sat behind the cash register, watching a small television while some modern African fusion music played in the background. I quickly roamed the three aisles, two of which were filled with foreign junk food, until I saw the spice shelf. I wondered how they could sell them so cheaply.

When I picked up the industrial-sized jar of bay leaves, Senator smirked. "What? I happen to be out of bay leaves, and this would cost three times as much at home," I reasoned.

Now he couldn't contain his laughter. "I buy cds on vacation; you buy spices. You are such a weirdsmobile!"

I smiled at the use of his ridiculous pet name for me. "Scoff now; you won't make fun of me when you are slurping delicious homemade soup!"

We walked into the restaurant next door, and the hostess quickly seated us at the only available table on the nonsmoking side. We were close to a local family with a baby. The mother was talking to the infant girl and amusing her while they waited for their dinner to come. All I could think to myself was, "Lady, if you keep talking to that baby that way, she's liable to grow up with a southern accent..."

The food was good and messy. Or maybe I was just messy. It's sort of a tradition whenever I go out for Mexican food. I have to drop a least one scoop of salsa on the menu. I do not do this on purpose, but it is a matter of poor logistics. The server places the chips and salsa in the center of the table, equidistant to all. My short arms and small hands grab a chip, dip excessively, and return the distance to my mouth. Meanwhile I am reading and contemplating which arrangement of cheese and tortillas is best. Inevitably, I dribble.

We concluded our meal and drove back to the hotel. As had become our pattern, we were in early. I wiggled my way through another two minute episode of Montgomery's local forecast, and then slid into bed next to Senator. It was comfortable enough, but I was starting to miss our bed. Alabama was sweet, but it was not home for us.

Thursday morning began with a short trip along the route determined by the conjoined wisdom of three different maps of Montgomery. None of them were exactly accurate. One was out of scale, but fairly functional in most parts. From the second, we gathered the general idea of the layout of the streets, although one was incorrectly labeled by two letters. The last of the triad was the most useful, but still failed to tell us that 'you can't get there from here'. We took a short trip and ended up in the labyrinth of a college campus. So now we were not only the dumb lost tourists; we were also the *old* dumb lost tourists.

When we accidentally found our way out of the maze, we came along easier to the stately brick four-square style home that had once belonged to F. Scott and Zelda Fitzgerald. Scott was best known for his fictional depiction of the United States during the Jazz Age, when anything went. Zelda was best known for being crazy, but what does one expect when one names one's child Zelda?

We approached the house and stepped into the foyer. There was confusion about this literary site. Some sources claimed it was a free museum, while others said that it was only a small portion of a building that was now divided into a handful of apartments. As it turned out, there were several apartments actively occupied by no one named Fitzgerald. The part devoted to the museum was tiny, and there was now a charge to get in. I declined, not for budgetary reasons so much as rip-off reasons. I was getting the same vibe that I received when we went to the crummy Poe home in Richmond. I decided it was enough just to be in the yard and outside the home, and so we left.

The next stop was much easier to find due to good downtown signage and a better meeting of the minds among the maps. While on the highway the day before, we saw one sign for the Confederate White House. I had no interest in seeing the current White House, but this one might actually be interesting. I guess I was unaware that Montgomery had ever served as the capital of the C.S.A..

We parked and fed the accompanying meter. It was approximately ten cents for thirty minutes. "You can tell Daley's not in charge here!"* We walked around the block to the entrance of the upper class, but not too showy, White House.

The font door was wide open, and no grumpy secret service men tried to corral us to the appropriate lines. In fact, a large group spilled out of the foyer and onto the sidewalk. We joined the rear of the group, straining to hear the entertaining and enthusiastic guide. She explained that Montgomery had served as the capital of the Confederate states prior to moving it to Richmond. Jefferson Davis, his wife Varina, and their children lived here for a while after his inauguration as the first and only President of the Confederacy.

Two stories in particular stand out in my mind, both pertaining to their children. We learned that one of their children died tragically in Richmond after falling from a balcony. We also learned that one of their children was an adopted black boy for whom Varina had fallen. This had to be a pretty radical move for the wife of a president who led so many slaveholding states.

It was no coincidence that the guide told us stories about children. When the large group squeezed in, we saw that we were the only childless Yankees who had found their way into a tour for local fourth graders and their parental chaperones. *No, we don't stick out or anything.* Overall, the children were well behaved, but that didn't keep me from breathing a sigh of relief when they announced that everyone had to get back to the bus.

In four minutes flat the home cleared out. Ten-year olds fled the scene, brushing past us with the occasional quickly muttered "'scuse me". I looked at Senator, glad to see that he had survived human contact with kids. It was as though we had just inherited the mansion ourselves.

---

*Mayor Daley of Chicago has jacked up parking fees so high that the author strongly recommends taking out a small loan before attempting to park in the Windy City.

The boards creaked as we walked up the stairs in silence. Civil War era clothing, personal items, furniture, and letters helped complete the picture of a troubled yet feisty people. When these items were in use, the hope of an independent South was still realistic. I have mixed feelings about the War Between the States, which I will not go into here. Nevertheless, at some point each U.S. citizen should carefully examine the bloody conflict from both sides. There are surprises to be found.

In keeping with our total immersion in the Deep South, we now moved on to the Hank Williams Museum. To understand the museum, you have to first understand that country singer Hank Williams falls only slightly short of a saint in the South. If the paperwork weren't being completed at a southern pace, he would likely have been canonized years ago. We were about to dive into the epicenter.

We drove down the block to find a parking spot. I handed Senator the change to feed the meter, but it wouldn't go past half an hour. "Well that won't work. We don't want to be rushed." We drove down a few spots to a different parking meter. The second meter ate far more than its share of coinage. "Now what's the deal?" Eventually we gave up and parked at a meter further away, losing more change for a half hour limit.

Hank Williams tunes surged as we approached the door. Inside, the guide greeted us and sold us our admission tickets. "What can you tell us about the parking meters," Senator started.

"Yeah, we keep trying to feed them, but we can't seem to get more than thirty minutes," I added.

She cheerfully began her rehearsed explanation. "Are you parked next to a red meter? Because if you are, you can only get thirty minutes on those. That's because the city doesn't want people taking up parking spots for too long in front of places like banks and the post office. Now the black meters are unlimited, but people don't necessarily have to feed them now because there's construction on the street and if you can squeeze in, you can park in the center section." She paused to peer outside and gesture toward the jumble of parked cars.

"There, where it says 'No Parking'?"

"Yes, but you can park there today." She read our bewilderment. "Of course, if you *do* get a ticket, it's only $4.00."

"$4.00?!"we asked in unison. That was laughable. Why didn't she just say that in the first place? With the complexities of legal parking behind us, we entered the museum.

The first exhibit to greet my eyes was the baby blue Cadillac in which Mr. Williams died. "I guess we're supposed to start from the other end," I observed.

"Good call," Senator said flatly. We watched the video on Hank's life and viewed several more exhibits. Thanks to the mannequins sporting his favorite stage suits, I gathered that Williams was a very thin man. I also gathered that he was not a very happy man. I think he might have known that he would not live to see old age. The museum was more engrossing than I had expected, holding my attention from start to finish. In general it can be described as bittersweet, right down to the 'Hanks for the memories' coasters in the gift shop.

It was early afternoon and time to hit the cowboy trail ourselves. We left Alabama and crossed into Mississippi from yet another direction. There is not much between the state line and Oxford, unless you are in search of Bingo Heaven. Contentedly situated along Route 78, despite the noticeable lack of towns, lies the bingo stretch. In a three mile span there are at least six bingo halls. These are not shabby little rooms that sporadically host the game; these are halls the size of car dealerships, with permanent B-I-N-G-O signs and plenty of parking, whose sole purpose is to welcome serious players.

It was actually a little creepy. The only other discernible industry was a gas station or two. I assumed these existed so patrons could fuel up after a long day on the bingoward road. I mean, where were all of these people coming from? Could they really play enough bingo to support healthy competition among several halls? More importantly, what kind of prizes were they giving away? I suppose it is also possible that it was a front for some seedier business. It's far more pleasant, however, to believe that somewhere in the middle of Mississippi, a place exists where time has less meaning than five letters and seventy-five numbers. Don't you agree?

Arriving in Oxford around 5:00pm meant we would have to wait until the next morning to see Faulkner's house. Though I would never claim to be an expert on his works, I feel that I at least rise to the level of Faulkner geek. For instance, I had been plotting to see his home for about seven years prior to our visit. For another instance, I once belonged to a book group that read only Faulkner books. Of course, there were only two and a half members, but greatness is rarely crowded.

We checked into a hotel, asking the desk attendant about the Thai restaurant next door. She said that it had just opened. That was good enough for us. When on vacation, be a pioneer. We walked in, were seated in a booth, and waited to order.

A dopey, hairy white boy took our drink order. He was generally confused, but Senator pointed out that he and the rest of the staff must be new. It was a reasonable point, so we were patient. A few moments later a girl took our order. After some time, Dopey brought our dinners out. Well, not exactly *our* dinners, but somebody's. "This isn't our food," Senator said, "Maybe it belongs to the table behind us." *Yeah, considering they're the only other people in here. The guy had a 50/50 shot...*

Here is where Dopey lost our good graces. "No, it says you ordered..." We stopped him right there. Wherever that sentence was going, we were positive we had not ordered chicken and shrimp. He insisted. We walked. Thus, we demolished yet another institution associated with our vacation.

The quest for eastern food continued, and we eventually found ourselves in an unadorned Indian restaurant. The polite young girl took our order, and we sat back to indulge in some fine Indian programming on the television in the dining room. It looked like a low- budget musical romance, with the main couple dancing around in slow motion before hopping into bed and singing some more. What a great country.

This time our food arrived in perfect translation, with mounds of delicious steamed vegetables and basmati rice, served with tasty curries. The chef came out to greet us personally and inquire about the food. When we raved about it, he went on to explain that his family loved that particular dish. They always make it in their "pray-sah gook-ah", which they schlepped with them all the way from India. It took me a few seconds to realize he was referring to his beloved pressure cooker. Hhmmm, we would have to keep that in mind.

Oxford is a college town with a college town square. To make the most of this hub of twentysomething night life, they have regulated traffic through a roundabout. This means that if you want to see all of the shops, restaurants, or bars surrounding the plaza, all you have to do is enter the circle and ride. In fact, you may get to see these same sites three or four times depending on the merging talents of the other drivers on the roundabout.

When we finally had a chance to exit, we left Trucky in search of a good cup of college-student-barista-brewed coffee. Square Books offered an outdoor balcony and a great latte. (The fact that they had an entire section devoted to Faulkner didn't hurt, either.) We selected our books and dropped off into our individual worlds. I am passionate about teaching, but places like this make me pine for my bookseller days.

Back at the hotel that night we discussed our options for the remainder of the trip. Friday morning we would visit the Faulkner home, and then we could either drive for a while and stop for the night, or marathon the eleven hours to get home. A lot would depend on the storm line that we had managed to keep missing for the past week. Around 1:00 in the morning the worst of it passed over our hotel. Loud, long rolls of thunder rocked the place, and lightening produced a strobe show that woke us up several times. By morning, it was cloudy but calm as we started off for Bill's house.

Rowan Oak, the home that William Faulkner occupied from the early 1930s until his death in the early 1960s, is one of those hidden gems that is surrounded by a neighborhood which keeps its secret well. What looked like a dead end was a small parking lot that bordered woods. Taking the easy trail, we crossed through the trees to three acres of meadows and gardens, and a tree-lined avenue. The path led us to the front door.

Inside we were greeted-- and I use the term loosely-- by a local college student who took our cash and gave us the brochure, explaining that the tour was self-guided. This, she believed, ended her duties as far as we were concerned. I wondered if she had even read a Faulkner novel all the way through. *Don't you have anything to add? Heck, even Benjy would have contributed some commentary!*

We shared our floor plan and read about the various rooms we were viewing. Upon acquiring the home, Faulkner spent a great deal of time refinishing it, tackling many home improvement projects. Senator's attention focused on the bookshelves Faulkner built. "Geez, those aren't anywhere near straight! I did a better job than that on ours," he proudly declared. That's not really what I had in mind when I thought of literary criticism of Faulkner...

Then again, no one can accuse Faulkner of being a gifted interior designer. The rooms are generally stark, simply furnished, and white, with the notable exception of his writing room. Here, the outline for his short story *A Fable* is written on the walls in his own handwriting. It is assumed that he was using a version of the storyboard technique he had picked up while working on screenplays in Hollywood. I tend to believe that he did it one day on a whim when he sat back and realized the drabness of his décor. Or maybe he was just drunk.

We finished our tour and roamed the grounds. A few outbuildings dotted the property. At one time there was a maze garden, but it has since disintegrated into concentric bunches of weeds. Still, the home and grounds were attractive and I could imagine sitting at a window and writing comfortably at Rowan Oak on a breezy spring day.

Once again we found ourselves on the interstate. We flipped on the radio. There were reports of deadly tornadoes that had touched down in Tennessee, Arkansas, and Missouri the night before. Our route home still traced the edge of the squall line, but we had evaded the danger. We drove for a few hours, and stopped for a fast sandwich. "We've really been making great time," I mentioned. "Would you like me to drive now?" I recognized the look in Senator's eye. It was the look of determination. It was the look of a man on a mission. That meant it was also the look of a man who was absolutely going to make it home tonight. "Fine by me," I responded to my own question.

In record time we were home. I was pleased that we had returned a night earlier than planned. It was like the opposite of sneaking out at night and hoping not to get caught. We were home and no one was the wiser. Our bed. Our bathroom. Our home.

Afterword

By spring of 2009, Senator and I had been together for six years, traveling more than 100 days during that time. Some trips were better than others, but none of them were boring. In fact, the best part of any trip is the feeling of running away together, sans commitments to anything but each other. The freedom that comes with the occasional break from jobs, housework, side projects, phones, and email is a necessary and exhilarating breath of fresh air. This is why you will never find a laptop among our luggage. So if you can't reach us, just leave a message after the beep. Eventually when we get home, we'll get back to you. Don't be surprised, though, if our minds wander back to a street in New York, a canyon in Arizona, or a beach in Wisconsin. Part of us has never left these places.

~Wendy V
May 2009

www.ingramcontent.com/pod-product-compliance
Lightning Source LLC
LaVergne TN
LVHW041628070426
835507LV00008B/503